THE CIRCUS
Bigger and Better than Ever?

THE CIRCUS
Bigger and Better than Ever?

Herb Clement

*The excitement, pulse, and pace of the circus
from both sides of the spotlights.*

SOUTH BRUNSWICK AND NEW YORK:
A. S. BARNES AND COMPANY
LONDON: THOMAS YOSELOFF LTD

A. S. Barnes and Co., Inc.
Cranbury, New Jersey 08512

Thomas Yoseloff Ltd
108 New Bond Street
London W1Y OQX, England

Library of Congress Cataloging in Publication Data

Clement, Herb.
  The circus, bigger and better than ever?

  1. Circus—United States.   I.   Title.
GV1803.C53   791.3′0973   73-106
ISBN 0-498-01321-9

*Unless otherwise noted, all photographs in this book are
by Arvid Zumwalt.*

PRINTED IN THE UNITED STATES OF AMERICA

FOR SLIM

NOTE: Circus Bartok, which figures heavily in this book, headed "for the barn" in July, 1972, and has remained inactive since that time.

CONTENTS

PREFACE

This book does not pretend to be a survey of the circus in America, or even an account of circuses that perform along the eastern seaboard—an area that I call home. It is primarily an account of my own involvement with several circuses, of what they mean to me, and of what their performers think, feel, and talk about.

Research on the run has been the keynote for gathering material found in this book. Throughout the Northeast, I have dropped everything and run to the circus whenever its presence was discovered. Together with my photographer friend I have spent many hours visiting with performers and managers, and ridden many miles in order to spend a few hours on circus lots and in arenas. Sometimes our reception has perplexed us, as was the case when we drove from New York City to Hartford, Connecticut, in order to visit the Hamid Morton Shrine circus—only to be welcomed by the Shriners and evicted by the late George Hamid at the same time!

Disappointments like those are the exception, rather than the rule, fortunately. For the most part, "front office men" have welcomed us into the complex, fast-paced world of the circus, aware that we may not always agree with them about their various offerings, but otherwise assured that we are on the side of the circus all the way.

If I had to pick a single word to describe the appeal of the circus to me, it would be *vibrancy*. The unique combination of sights, sounds, and smells that characterize the circus seem, somehow, to lump together into that one word. Everything about a circus—its animals, performers, musicians and workers—seems injected with vibrancy when a show "clicks" and really takes off into a winning performance. It is this euphoric, shot-of-adrenalin feeling that transmits to spectators as well. I have tried to remember this while assimilating technical facts about circuses, or while listening to the life stories of performers as they have recounted their histories to me. I have tried to keep my eye on my own childhood, when I first entered a circus arena intoxicated by the heady smells of jungle beasts and stunned by the magnetic appeal of circus rings domed by vast, glittering spider webs of aerial rigging.

The circus seems to be a magically confusing world where the borderline between reality and illusion is obscured by a dazzling profusion of exotic sensations. It affects me now as it did years ago; and I confess, without the least trace of embarrassment, that I am, after all, one of those *"Children of all ages!"*

ACKNOWLEDGMENTS

I gratefully express my thanks to the hundreds of performers in several circuses for their whole-hearted cooperation, as well as their enthusiasm concerning this book. Similarly, thanks are due to Ringling Bros. Circus officials Irvin Feld, president and producer, and Allen Bloom, senior vice president and director of promotion and sales. Charley Baumann, performance director of Ringling's Blue Unit, has also been most helpful, as have been Roy Zinser of the Clyde Beatty-Cole Bros. Circus, Milton, Betty, and Bunni Bartok together with Jan Perz of Circus Bartok, Wilson Storey of Sells and Gray Circus, Hoxie Tucker and Jon Hall of Hoxie Bros. Circus, and Harry Rawls of King Bros. Circus.

My thanks to Joseph Sclafani, publisher of the *Staten Island Register,* for permission to include biographical data and descriptions of circus-act routines that were printed by that newspaper.

The public relations firm of Solters, Sabinson and Raskin has also been most helpful. Early in my interviews with performers it was that firm's Jack Ryan who allowed me free reign backstage to obtain interviews when performers were momentarily unhurried.

I could hardly list thanks without citing the importance of Arvid Zumwalt, whose photographs virtually fill this book. It was he who carted me all over the Northeast from one circus to another, often in weather that was close to unendurable, taking time that was not always his to give.

Important editorial assistance was given me by Al McGrigor, whose nagging often forced necessary deletions, and whose cool head often kept me from losing mine.

Further editorial assistance, in addition to manuscript typing, was extended by Veronica Nelson, for which she has my undying gratitude.

General information and biographical data cannot always be dragged from the archives of one's memory. Therefore I should like to thank Curtis Brown, Ltd. for permission to use data originally published in *The Big Top,* by Fred Bradna as told to Hartzell Spence. Similar permission was extended by "Chappie" Fox, author of the book *A Pictorial History of Performing Horses,* published by the Superior Publishing Company, Seattle. For data about Grock I am indebted to the firm of Mundus Verlag, Stuttgart, which published that clown's autobiography under the title of *Nit M-o-o-o-glich* in 1956.

If all of the people who helped bring this book about were assembled together, they would undoubtedly make up a circus of considerable size. I cannot thank each individual here, but I hope that they will have that special feeling of pride when they take this book from the shelf, knowing that they, too, are part of it.

THE CIRCUS
Bigger and Better than Ever?

1

BRADNA BLEW THE WHISTLE

IN 1937, my Uncle Arthur lured me from the suburbs of Boston, Massachusetts, led me by the hand onto a rickety Boston and Maine railroad coach, and, after a twenty-minute ride, deposited me in the upper-story level of the North Station where he plunked me soundly in a seat at Boston Garden. The Ringling Brothers and Barnum & Bailey Circus was playing there for its customary week in May. From that euphoric moment my life has been a drastically altered thing.

The sawdust was the color of wood, not the dyed stuff of later years. The rings were red. The bandstand, over the entrance to the hippodrome track, was bedecked with bunting and glittered with exciting flashes of brass and silver as the band instruments reflected the glare of the floodlights.

Circus workers ambled about in the arena, checking rigging and tugging at rope stays that held the center ring arena cage upright. Some played cards. A feeling of calm seemed to prevail in that incredibly vast space, so choked with ropes and other circus paraphernalia.

But the memory of the moment that remains indelibly fixed today is not one of sight but of smell. The odor that filtered into the arena from backstage (where a huge menagerie was kept) shot through me. The tangy, spunky odor of lions and tigers mingled alluringly with the forthright, haylike odor of hooved stock of many lands. A pall of horse odor hung like a blanket, superimposed by the very special ammonia scent that belonged to elephants. Ringling carried fifty of them in those days, and the aroma of elephant was everywhere.

The enormous curtains that closed the entrance were bright red. They billowed into the arena whenever the back doors were opened in the menagerie, revealing glimpses of performers and equipment that drove me wild with excitement. Exotic flags with glinting brass flagpole adornments were carried casually back and forth by persons in weird, colorful attire. A horse, probably white, pranced nervously in the backstage gloom, his trappings all but concealing his body. Sitting astride him was a rider lost in the maze of glitter and color of many moving bodies, both animal and human. On either side of the horse hung copper kettledrums, bedecked with dyed rope and long tassels.

Then something happened. A gentleman in a red coat, wearing a black hat and black pants, with spotlessly shined shoes that gleamed all the way to the second balcony, stepped into the arena. He did not advance to the center ring, as I had expected him to do. Instead, he stepped quietly before the curtains and walked over to one of the circus workers, to whom he spoke briefly. The worker, galvanized into action, hurried to the opposite end of the arena and untangled a single strand of rope. (I learned much later that the man who had sent the worker on this detail was Fred Bradna, dean and most famous of equestrian directors.)

Bradna stood very still. His hawklike, squinting eyes took in every feature and every fault in the arena setup. Everything—absolutely everything—must be in exactly the correct position. No line must hang differently. No rope must lie coiled two feet from where it had been coiled before the preceding performance. Every elephant tub must be stacked in precisely the same manner. Every prop, no matter how incidental, must be in its proper place; every performer must be ready for the opening "spec"—in his correct place, completely costumed before Bradna would begin a performance. He gave the impression of being a hard man (which he was) and atrociously cruel (which he was not) while he stood there, alone, quietly magnetizing every spectator's gaze as he surveyed the entire garden without moving from his position.

The curtains remained slightly parted during these tense moments. I learned much later that this was arranged in order that Bradna could keep his eye on Myrtle, a remarkable elephant that Bradna claimed could sense that proper moment when the opening spec should begin even better than he could himself! When Myrtle swung her ears forward and leaned into her first step, shifting her great volume and mass into that peculiarly aquatic glide that characterizes a perambulating elephant—that was the time when Bradna blew his whistle and the goliath of a show lifted its great weight and gathered momentum, sparking and glittering as it began with a brash, energetic parade around the hippodrome.

I felt so lost and forlorn, sitting in my seat beside Uncle Arthur. Why didn't *I* belong to such an exciting world? Why must I live in drab surroundings, with people who wore clothes of no color, who never smiled much, and who went about workaday chores with a glumness that could only be described as New Englandesque? But these qualifications were only momentary, for I couldn't afford to miss the excitement at hand. I would, after all, have to make use of this vibrancy for a full year before it came my way again! I sat transfixed, mesmerized by the tension of the moment.

The casual action that Mr. Bradna next performed increased my anxiety a thousandfold, if that was possible. If anyone had spoken to me at that moment I would almost certainly have snapped and shattered into fragments. Mr. Bradna glanced toward the backstage area and grasped the shiny brass whistle that hung around his neck on a black ribbon. His white gloved hand held the whistle about half way from his chest to his chin. His left hand elevated slightly, its index finger pointing directly towards the entrance—*that* entrance, behind which all of those exotic sights and smells were congregated, and all of those talented, beautiful people and animals strained and champed at the bit. They were catching the excitement of the audience as the murmurs of expectation rose.

Then, unaccountably, the murmurs of the audience and the volume of hushed voices dropped to leave a vacuum of anticipation that was strangely, eerily silent. The tension was so high that the air seemed to crackle.

In a flash it happened. Bradna placed the whistle to his lips and a piercing blast cut the air. The red curtains swirled apart. The arena was plunged into a cloudburst of deep blue floodlights as the entrance was bathed in white and amber spots. Trumpets, trombones, and tubas flashed and gleamed, and flags were swung upright. The hollow thunder of drums ached in my stomach as the procession spewed forth before me—an incredible display of excess that left me limp as it stepped into the arena like a conglomerate of gods from Olympus. The words that blared from the loudspeaker sent shivers through me then as they do to this day: "Children of all ages! Ringling Brothers and Barnum & Bailey Circus proudly presents . . . . ."

2
PULSE

IN THE 1950s I attended a dress rehearsal of the Ringling Bros. Circus in Madison Square Garden, New York.

I wandered into the arena as the parade, or "spec," was being walked through its paces. No music was played. A bone-tired file of performers plodded wearily around the hippodrome track as riggers made hurried adjustments to complicated aerial rigging overhead, shouting back and forth to one another as they worked. The intricately clogged paraphernalia high above the arena floor seemed like a vast trap net, ready to drop on the paraders below.

An elephant in the procession balked, creating a momentary bottleneck.

"Take it easy, Ruth," said a calm voice into the public address system. The elephant obeyed. "Annie, hold your arms a little higher," said the voice. "Remember, you will be wearing real feathers. Now if all you girls will keep your arms high, and not drag your feathers on the ground, we can have a really beautiful number here." The girls stared glumly at the sawdust. They would hold their arms high when they wore their feathers and not before, obviously.

Clearly audible over the loudspeaker were several words spoken in the background. "OK Merle. As soon as the girls exit." Silence, as the girls sloughed out of the arena behind Ruth, who inquisitively poked at nearby props while she padded towards the dark, cavernous backstage area. Then the voice again—"OK? OK Merle."

At the corner bandstand a stocky man was explaining something to an organist. He turned casually to the drummer and made little circular gestures with his right hand, descriptive, I thought, of a particular effect. The man issuing the instructions was Merle Evans, famed conductor of the Ringling Bros. Circus band. In his left hand he held a silver cornet.

What occurred next was magic. Shifting the cornet to his right hand, Evans nodded to the man at the microphone, lifted the instrument to his lips, and slivered the air with a shattering cascade of sound. Galvanized into fervent support, the band gamely accompanied him. It was an Evans fanfare, known throughout the world as the *ne plus ultra* of fanfares.

What followed it could hardly have mattered less. It was undoubtedly the customary string of chromos that comprised the basic music of Ringling spectacles in the 1950s, tied together with fantastic key changes and arrangements that were pure Evans. The finale of these musically Disney-esque spectacles consisted of tunes that were ever more exciting and majestic. It reached its climax at the precise point when the last yard of sequined train on the last elephant blanket disappeared behind the crimson curtains, and the arena was left in semidarkness, its audience literally gasping with spent, emotional energies.

Gabrielli, William Walton, and Stravinsky notwithstanding, it is generally conceded that Evans is a foremost composer of fanfares.

Again the curtains opened and again the performers entered, obviously annoyed at submitting themselves to the indignity of walking to the accompaniment of nursery tunes. But this time their steps quickened as they filed onto the hippodrome track. Their faces brightened. Arms were held high—as if they really wore those vaunted feathers. The entire assemblage *bounced* into the arena. Even the recalcitrant Ruth, enlivened by the brisk tempo, glided along bobbing her head, her inquisitive trunk no longer involved in the elephantine skullduggery of yanking at ropes or tipping over toolboxes.

A whistle shrilled the cast to a halt and silenced the band.

"Now listen, everybody," the loudspeaker said, "this is the place where we have the bubbles. Tony! Tony? Can we have a few bubbles up there to show them what it's like?" (Several machines whirred high overhead, and bubbles drifted down to the arena floor.) "Now I want you all to raise your hands high overhead when you hear this fanfare. Play it for them, will you Merle?"

A deep roll on the tom-toms and a triple-tongued ripple of chromatics ended in a shivering cymbal crash as a ponderous theme, played by tubas and trombones, began.

"There. That's it. Now that doesn't come anywhere else in the spec. Only with the bubbles. When you hear it, lift your arms slowly into the air and keep walking in time with the music. Got it? OK, Merle, let's start at the bubble music again."

At the first beat of the fanfare Ruth swung her cardboard ears forward and began to shuffle along in the midst of the performers. The fanfare glittered. The performers marched slowly, their arms elevated as if in supplication to an invisible god; while above, bubble machines buzzed and ground, releasing millions of rainbow-hued bubbles until the arena was awash with them.

I am not unaware of the trumpery and ersatz glamor that is involved in the production of a circus spectacle. But sitting there, I was impressed. In my mind's eye I could envision the moment that this combination of sights and sounds would create. Housewives across America, accompanied by their glassy-eyed children and harried spouses, would consider this garish, blatant, and utterly uncouth display of excess as one of the most beautiful and affecting moments of their lives. Perhaps they would be right.

The theme didn't matter. It could have been Romeo and Juliet, Cinderella, the Seasons, Signs of the Zodiac, Birthdays, or anything at all. Somehow, they all turn out the same in any case. The theme is not the point. The emotional impact of

sight, sound, and smell that surrounds it is what matters. This impact is not delivered by the visual theme, nor by the expensive and often ludicrous costumes or theatrical effects. It is born through the pulse beneath these fripperies—the music. It is the band. It is Merle Evans.

1969 was Evans's last year as bandmaster for Ringling Bros. Circus. By season's end he had conducted over thirty thousand performances. Most circus fans, at that time, could not remember a time when he did not lead the band, except during an abortive squabble between the circus management and the musicians' union. During that time Evans was "replaced" by a bandmaster who was well equipped to conduct outdoor music for fairs and sporting events, but who had no "sense of feel" for the tightly organized precision of the Ringling show. The music of Evans's substitute razzled but it didn't dazzle. Happily, the difficulty between management and union was resolved, and Ringling got its heartbeat back.

As simple as it is effective, an Evans accompaniment made many an ordinary act exceptional. It was Evans who first produced the spine-chilling, ascending chromatic chords that accompanied Harold Alzana as he staggered on his precarious route up a thirty-five-degree tightwire and flippantly walked the rails of the second balcony to land on the tiny platform from which he finally began his high wire "turn." What better musical accompaniment than to play a descending scale of those same, chromatic chords as Alzana descended? The effect was miraculous.

Evans premiered Stravinsky's "Circus Polka" written expressly for Ringling's 1942 elephant act. The music, often performed today and available on recordings, was the only new aspect of the elephant production number, which was otherwise substantially the same routine that had been performed for years before. The addition of tutus that hung like dirty, limp rags from the elephants, was not enough to turn the act into a new feature. All that remains of that act is its riotous score, originally played by Evans and his band, with its interpolations of the soldier's chorus from *Faust,* suitably deharmonized by Stravinsky in order to turn the whole thing into a massive satire.

The genius of an Evans score is not to be found at its best in music for parades, finales, or aerial spectaculars. It is most evident in the music played for the turns performed by the artists themselves, for here there may be a dozen or more quick changes of tempo as a horse changes its gait, an

Merle Evans and his cornet. (Courtesy Circus World Museum, Baraboo, Wisconsin)

acrobat reaches the high point of a feat, or an elephant mounts a tub. As feline performers are notoriously balky, they are particularly tricky to accompany. A tune that may last only thirty seconds in one performance (as a tiger rolls over, for instance) may last several minutes during another show if the animal is obstinate. The score must be extended to cover the delay, and it must be "padded" on the spot.

I have watched Evans closely during these critical moments. Always he was the same. He looked directly at the ring, his back turned to the band. Sometimes he beat time with his left hand, or held it suspended in the air as the band played. When the feat was accomplished, he turned to the band but made no visible signal as the music changed to a different tempo in preparation for the next routine. I still can't tell how he did it.

The fact that one often forgot the presence of the band during a circus performance was testi-monial to Evans's talent. The pulse of the under-scoring music was so remarkably at one with the action in the rings that the total effect was of a single entity. Always, when a flyer completed his twist and smacked securely, wrist to wrist, with his catcher, there was musical emphasis that turned the action into an event. Hearts in the audience, caught in momentary fear as the flyer was in free flight, settled gratefully back into their proper chest cavities accompanied by the thump of a bass drum at the end of the snare drum's roll. Immediately the casual, fluid lilt of a waltz was resumed and the audience prepared for its next, vicarious swing through space.

By using themes adapted from all levels of musical composition, from classical to popular, and by writing music himself when nothing else sufficed, Merle Evans created, borrowed, and stole the perfect complement to hundreds of different circus routines throughout each two-hour-and-forty-five-minute performance. But the effect was not one of bits and pieces. Rather, the end result from this incredible mishmash was unity. Audiences left the auditorium glutted with the excess of sight, sound, and smell that comprises the circus. It was too much. It was not enough. It was the circus; the only place where, it has been said, one traditionally gets too much for his money.

Long after the show had left town, when the arena had shed its sparkling circus magnificence and had reverted to the comparatively drab euphoria of basketball games and trade shows, the memory of that tingling circus sound remained. The dark reaches of the arena seemed to retain the faint echo of a fanfare, the rattle of a drum-roll, and the dulcet glide of the flyers' waltz.

It was the Evans sound. The pulse of the circus. The sound that brought them back next year.

3

TIGER MAN

KETTLEDRUMS rolled. A white spotlight stabbed the dark arena and struck a mirrored ball, sending fragments of reflection bouncing into the far reaches of the auditorium. A massive Bengal tiger sat on its hind legs atop the ball, and the music built to a triumphant climax. The ball slowly revolved, the tiger turning with it, while a snowstorm of reflections swirled in the arena. It was a characteristic feature of the Ringling Bros. Circus, and one of the most dramatic moments of pure circus in the history of the circus itself.

"The revolving tiger and the one that jumps across the arena in short hops on its hind legs— the hind-leg tiger—are two of the most difficult routines in my act," said Charly Baumann, master tiger trainer of the Ringling show, during a backstage interview at New York's Madison Square Garden. "To get a tiger to jump onto a stool is nothing," he continued. "But a tiger must have something solid to stand on. When you turn on the switch and the stool revolves, most tigers would panic, or want to get off. To have a tiger turn a full circle in a sitting-up position, especially with all of those reflections confusing it, is not an easy thing to do."

"How did you figure out how to do it?" I asked naively.

"Well, nobody's gonna tell you how, that's for sure. You have to figure it out for yourself."

"Sorry. I promise not to ask again," I added lamely.

"That's all right. I wouldn't tell you anyway!"

Baumann runs the largest tiger act in the world currently, and keeps the number in his troupe of performing felines between ten and twelve.

He was brought into the difficult and exotic business of animal training by none other than Willy Hagenback, of Germany. It was Hagenback who introduced the gentle school of animal training (and who also introduced into zoos the modern, moated animal enclosures that have replaced barred cages). Under his famous mentor, Baumann first worked lions ("easy to work with because they have a family life, and are used to one another"), then polar bears (no comment), and finally tigers. He began in 1950 and joined Ringling in 1957.

Throughout the act, Kismet, Baumann's favorite, sits away from the other tigers. When her trainer walks too close the tiger grabs him around the shoulders and licks his face. Explaining this routine, Baumann revealed that Kihmet has but one eye. When she was born her mother turned on her and tried to kill her, biting out an eye.

"I fought the mother off and took the little cub to my trailer, all wet and yowling. I kept her in the trailer for eighteen months. She was housebroken, and a perfect pet. I didn't want to train her, but she got too rough on the furniture; you can imagine! When I was going to perform in Moscow I lost a tiger. Under my contract I had to appear with eight tigers; so I stuck Kismet into the act just to sit there. I came too close one time and she grabbed me and licked me all over. I must say it was a frightening thing because it had never happened before, and in front of all those people! But the Moscow audience loved it, and thought that it was part of the act. So I began to train Kismet to do the trick the way *I* wanted her to and it has been in the act ever since."

At the time of Baumann's conversation with me, Kismet was in heat. The trainer had to be careful because the tigress didn't want to have anything to do with him. ("She's in love with a big male tiger to her left; not with me!") Actually, three of his tigers were in heat at that time. All was quiet, but Baumann expected that in a few days, when the heat had passed and the animals had not been bred, they would become cantankerous and, not surprisingly, dangerous as well. Complicating matters was the problem of reintroducing a tiger named Natasha, who had been out of the act, ill, for three weeks. Baumann must be aware of the proper moment when she could be allowed to take her place in the routine once more.

"If you show a tiger that no harm will come to him; then, in a little while, he actually gets to like working in the ring. But tigers are difficult because they start out not liking anybody—even their own brothers and sisters. They are solitary; but soon they become used to it, and then like it."

I had mixed thoughts as our brief conversation ended. I had the distinct feeling that they "got to like it" because of the firm but patient boss who coaxed and lured them to perform. In fact, the formula must be successful when applied to any animal act. Talented pupils plus brilliant boss equals amazing act.

In addition to his performance in the ring, which Baumann whittles and hones toward perfection constantly, the trainer assumed the duties of assistant performance director with Ringling's Blue Unit when it was formed in 1969. He accepted the post for several reasons. He thrives on circus life, and has both respect and love for the circus as an institution. In his European career he had been a circus director—a title that carries a different meaning in Europe, as far as total involvement in the circus is concerned, than it does in America. Lastly, it seemed to him that there was a future on the Ringling show. His availability—"I am around anyway, so I might as well do something"—and extra cash helped to settle the question. Ringling officials reveal that Baumann was hired as performance director for his ability, dedication and devotion to the circus. They feel that he brings a wealth of knowledge to the company.

Baumann's assessment of his own performance as assistant director is typically realistic. He dis-

Baumann's tiger act is one of the most beautiful seen in years.

cussed his role while getting ready for a performance in his dressing room.

Stripping off his shirt, he revealed a long scar on the right side of his chest and an enormous tiger tooth on a chain around his neck.

"The first thing I did was to hire Bob Harrison as my assistant. This is because of the mountains of paper work in the job of performance director now. You wouldn't believe it! It almost requires a full-time secretary. Bob is often with me watching the show, and when I goof off (once in a great while I like to take a quick look at a hockey game on TV) he is usually out there in the arena then, too. He has work to do during the show, like when he guides the stiltwalker around the hippodrome track so that the man won't hit guy wires or make a false step. When it comes to paper work he sometimes does it at night and sometimes during the day, in the morning. I knew Bob from earlier, and knew his capabilities; and it has worked out fine."

Baumann arranged his cummerbund with some difficulty. "They call me rough and I *am* a rough guy. But I am that way because some people take advantage of rules that we have. If you don't put your foot down once in a while you end up with no people—or just a bunch of guys who run around there and do whatever they feel like, and that's no show."

I suggested that the need for organization was what he was talking about.

"Right," Baumann agreed, "you have to have that. All right, sometimes you have to look the other way, and circumstances sometimes intervene. You have to make allowances. When something like that happens, you just grit your teeth and remember to look into the trouble next time."

"What are some of the actual duties involved in the position?" I asked the burly German.

Taking a handkerchief from his pocket, Bau-mann set it on the bench beside him. He donned gleaming, patent leather shoes with the help of a shoe horn. He then spat upon the handkerchief and polished the shoes as he spoke.

"I help in establishing the running order of the show in rehearsals in Venice, Florida. Then, after we are out on the road, I must see that the quality of the production is still the same as it was back in Venice, or even to improve it. I mean by this production numbers, not the contents of the acts. This is partly involved with costs; because, if we run late or slow, the costs can mount enormously. Then I also lay out the dressing rooms when we are on tour."

"That must be difficult in arenas that are less well equipped than Madison Square Garden," I ventured.

"Even here at the Garden; because there are only eight rooms available for a hundred and sixty-five performers."

He threw on his jacket, and shook himself into it.

An informal moment between Baumann and his beasts.

"But the worst is when an act can't go on, and I don't know until almost too late. Last week we had an act that came to me and said 'we can't make it' five minutes before it was supposed to. This is in spite of the fact that we are supposed to have an act ready when one is performing. Hell breaks loose then. Bob and I run all over the building, getting another act ready. Mostly the performers count on those that go before them to appear as scheduled—and mostly they do. But sometimes a performer is in as many as six appearances, what with specs, animals to get ready and other things that he does. Once in a while there isn't time to be ready a whole act before a performer has to go on. So if there is a sudden change in the program, the first thing is to determine what is the next act to go in. Then you tell the band, prop hands, lighting director. All these people, and more, too, have to be informed in the matter of a minute; so Bob and I, we gotta do a rush job. What you do is run by the band leader and say 'Hey! That act is out!'—and he knows to go on to the next one. Sometimes we stretch a clown walkaround out a little bit, until I give the cue that we are ready for the next routine. It's really something!"

Sitting quietly in the background during all of this talk was Bob Harrison, who occasionally pecked at his typewriter at the same time he was listening to the conversation. Finally he could restrain himself no longer and spoke up.

"If you'll excuse the interruption, I'd just like to say this. The role of performance director with Ringling Bros. Circus is roughly akin to that of stage manager in a theatrical production. In a factory, if you want to make the parallel, the role would be that of plant manager—plus personnel manager. Charly's role, when an act fails to appear, is similar to that of a plant manager when a machine breaks down or the sudden cancellation of an order occurs."

Baumann nodded agreement, and looked at his watch.

"He is right. And if I don't get outta here we are apt to have a machinery breakdown right here! Talk to Bob a little bit; but I've gotta get out there."

Polished to perfection, Baumann brushed imaginary dust from his sleeves, glanced briefly at his gleaming shoes, and was gone.

Turning to Bob Harrison, I offered a markedly loaded comment.

"You know, Bob," I said, "talking with Charly for some time now, I've come to the conclusion that he isn't personally anywhere nearly as difficult as he says he is."

Harrison, who had been looking at me over the top of his glasses, removed them and said, "Charly is a professional. He is a good, all-round, one-hundred-percent circus man. Now, my own background has been in industry, as a personnel manager; and if I had to be the one to select the right man for the job of performance director, Charly would be the one. He's a purist and a thoroughist, and he wants things run correctly. All you have to do is follow along with what he wants, and he is very easy to get along with. His background is Germanic. He has a heavy voice and a heavy manner; and the way he speaks sometimes doesn't rub people the right way. But everybody's different; and you have to take that into consideration."

"I agree," I added, "but I have been one of that breed of towners distastefully called a 'lot louse' for three years now at Ringling Bros. Circus in New York; and I have found the little comments about Baumann as an impossible person to be—shall we say—highly colored and prejudiced at the basis of things."

"You are right. They are often highly personal. It is like complaining about someone because you don't like the way they comb their hair! Well, you are not going to get rid of a performance director because you don't like his hairdo. Baumann produces, and that is what counts. The show is the most important thing. No getting around it."

The clatter of clogs as performers passed the dressing room, and the thump of the drum, told us that the show had started. Harrison put his glasses back on, peered at me and shrugged. He was right—the show had begun, and he had work to do. The show *was* the important thing. We left together, and only parted when he turned to go into the arena, where colors shimmered and spangles flashed. I left by the back door to emerge on Thirty-second Street, where life, if nearly as frenzied as that in the arena, was far less exciting and frequently downright dull.

4

MUD SHOW

SMOULDERING IN the heat left over from the broiling day, the people of small-town America sit on their front porches with nothing to do on this particular sultry evening. The icy, blue-white eye of television jumps and skitters in their parlors, unwatched. In town there is perhaps a bowling alley, a bar, and a single movie theater, but there is nothing novel, nothing different. With a sigh, the weary citizens turn in early.

But they awaken to a hamlet transformed, as the early glint of sunlight strikes a gaudy poster, tacked to the dilapidated side of a neighbor's barn. Similar advertisements, their colors screaming, hang in the windows of the local market, barber shop, and gas station; and the weekly newspaper carries a single column advertisement that further whets the appetites of the townsfolk for the event that is to take place.

The circus is coming!

Mistakenly thought dead in the 1960s, this dearly loved American institution visits many such towns once yearly. Though struggling for survival, it is very much alive, and brings to countless audiences the spark, vitality, color, and excitement that is much needed after months of drudgery and dullness on the farm, at the plant, or in the office.

Contrary to the belief created when Ringling stopped performing in tents and took to arenas, the tented circus is not dead at all in America. Many circuses still perform under canvas. The Clyde Beatty-Cole Bros. Circus, for instance, is the largest of these, and in 1969 it plugged its way over a 13,000-mile tour, performing to audiences estimated at two million people. Circus Bartok,

a one-ring circus like those in Europe, traveled 6493 miles in 1970.

These facts represent more than mileage. They tell of broiling, dust-caked days under a merciless sun, and swampy, soggy lots under many a deluge. They represent days of bone-cracking work and hours of heartache. But they also represent freedom.

In order to understand the problems involved in the production of a small circus, I became friends with Milton and Betty Bartok and their daughter and son-in-law, Bunni and Jan Bartok-Perz, the family unit under which Circus Bartok operates.

It is a beautiful but sometimes bedraggled circus, and lives up to its nickname of "Mud Show" as it sogs and leaks along its route in driving storms, rarely missing a date. Its tent, with a seating capacity of 2000, is usually battered within a month from the time the show leaves its winter quarters in Florida. The massive generators that supply power for the show were built in the 1930s and were said to be the oldest operating on the road in 1970.

Ignoring the odds, as do most circuses, Bartok blossoms like a queen, resplendent in its red, white, and green-striped sidewalls and white tent top. Given a beautiful day and a good lot, it becomes what it should be—a circus, not a show. When its six elephants jog into the ring, 2000 voices roar a welcome. When a single juggler manipulates his flaming torches, every eye is on him. They do not wander over three rings and two stages of similar feats, but watch a solitary performer, fascinated. Such concentration, on the part of the audience, results in a deeper understanding and appreciation of the performer's skill than is possible in multi-ring shows. Members of the audience begin to realize what goes into a performance, to learn what is exceptional and what is not. An act presented without style under these circumstances is lost before it begins. Performers, aware that their few minutes in the ring represent moments of glory, know this. It is a rare circus artist who does not make the most of it if he is the center of attraction.

Directly after he had purchased the circus, Doc Bartok made a daring alteration in its format. He reduced it from three rings to one.

"I did it for two reasons," he explained over coffee in his gleaming trailer. "I didn't have enough money to stock three rings continuously, and I didn't have three heads to watch everything that goes on in a three-ring circus!"

An added benefit was that of space requirements. Circus Bartok can fit into a lot no bigger than 250 by 450 feet, while a three-ring circus takes up much more space. This fact has permitted Circus Bartok to perform where larger shows cannot, and to tap formerly untouched revenue as a result.

Bartok's single ring is surrounded by reserved seat chairs, behind which seat wagons unfold to carry bleachers to the eaves of the tent. The customers' entrance on one side of the tent is opposed by a tunnel-like performers' entrance on the other. Extending to the ring curb and hung with a spangled curtain, the performers' entrance also supports the circus band overhead. It is a structure common to many European circuses, but virtually ignored in America, and gives the tent interior a festive appearance.

It also gives Bartok management difficulty in retaining bandsmen. Stationed atop the structure at the eaves of the tent, they are continually assaulted by either stultifying heat or chilly drizzle from leaks in the top.

On one occasion in Plainfield, New Jersey, the band, reduced through hardship to a trumpet and a drum, thumped gamely on while the trumpeter played music with his left hand and held an umbrella over his head with his right! During the performance thunderstorms caused the tent to leak and weaken. Outside in the mire a heavy trailer truck was brought around to the rear. The big top's guy ropes were hitched to it, pulled taut,

Circus Bartok mailbox at winter quarters was painted by a man called Popcorn, and is a masterpiece of folk art.

and the rig was driven slowly away from the tent, returning it to its correct, upright position. Inside, the audience was ignorant of the difficulty. It sat enthralled beneath a sea of umbrellas as the Fournasari clown family frantically performed an extended routine *ad lib*. The whole episode was carried on against a counterpoint of mud and a virtual deluge outside, which only became apparent when the elephants came into the ring, drenching the audience with rivers of water that streaked from their hides as they entered.

Jan Perz, manager of Circus Bartok and trainer of its animals, stood with me beneath a backyard awning. He squinted through rain-spattered eyes at the lot, which had become a swamp within minutes.

"Ees hard, dis life. But yaknow? What happen here, wid allda rain an leaky tent an ropes dat come out an all, ees not so unusual. A very show has dat, not only us. An den you wunda why da keeds start out to work for us an den leave. Ees hard. Ees too hard for dem. I don blame dem."

Perz knows what he is talking about when he speaks of hard work. It is under his direction and through much of his muscle power that the show is virtually rebuilt every winter. During the 1970 tour he managed the entire circus, trained and presented both the elephant act and the bear act, helped set up the tents, collected reserved seat tickets, and joined with others in the teardown of the show after each day's performances. He loaded and unloaded the entire menagerie—elephants and all. Traveling from one spot to another, he drove his own van containing the bears and their performance equipment. His wife drove their large house trailer.

It was also during the summer of 1970, when I traveled with Circus Bartok, that I learned the reason behind the weary smiles of most circus performers; I met a performer named Ryzard.

His act was a hand-balancing turn atop a high ladder. Perched precariously on his hands, his feet pointing to the tent top, he caught wooden bricks that were thrown to him from below, shifting his weight so that he teetered momentarily on one hand. By shifting his weight and piling the bricks alternately, he eventually built a fair-sized pile on the ladder's end.

Stripped to the waist, he cut a handsome figure high overhead, and flaunted his prowess in typical, "show-biz" style, apparently enjoying every moment of his act. The exhausting, upside-down routine was often performed in the one-hundred-degree heat that was trapped beneath the roof of the tent.

Ryzard was also in charge of setting up seats in the big top. He was aided by a small crew of local, one-day helpers who placed the seats around the ring; but he actually did most of the work

Sorting through electrical paraphernalia under the broiling sun before the Bartok season begins.

Popcorn applies his magic touch to a trailer.

himself. During my stay with the show, when temperatures rose to the high nineties, I watched him look over the job that the local worthies had done. Dissatisfied, he moved the entire placement of seats, ring, and assorted props to a point not more than three feet to the right, so that the whole arrangement was centered correctly in the tent. Ahead of him that day were two performances and the exhausting labor of taking down the tents together with all of their equipment, loading it into trucks and driving the vehicles to the next location, where everything would be set up all over again.

Watching him loosen iron stakes with a sledgehammer after the evening was over, I could well understand the grinding misery of one-a-day road life. He wore Levis that were once white but were now the color of mud, and sneakers. His torso, covered with mosquito bites, was gleaming with sweat and his hair was plastered to his head, soaked. His dungarees too, were soaked, and clung to him as if he had just come from a dip in some nearby pond.

I started to ask why he was involved in such arduous work, probably earning no more than the average office secretary, but somehow the question seemed pointless to me. It seemed silly for a "towner" like myself to confront a stranger and ask him to justify the work he had chosen. My words stopped just after I had begun the question with the word "why."

Ryzard needed no more. "Because," he said as he gestured to the ladder on which he had performed. (It stood by the open door of the van, waiting to be packed away.) It was a good answer.

Ryzard defected from a Polish circus troupe sent to this country to perform with another circus. Polish security agents traveled with the artists and were responsible for an attempt to remove him bodily from the lot in winter quarters when he joined Circus Bartok, but troupers fought them off. Earlier, his brother, prepared to flee Poland, was caught before he could escape from that country and has never been heard from since.

When he arrived at Circus Bartok as a defector, Ryzard was following a pattern set by others;

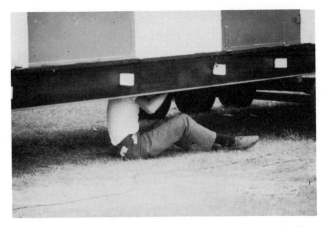

Under a seatwagon is sometimes the only cool place to work.

the show is known all over the world as a haven for circus people. In 1971 it adopted the policy of giving shelter to defectors from communist governments. It did this by assigning circus agents to free world, European countries. Once out of their communist homelands, performers signed with Circus Bartok on the spot and were allowed working visas to the United States because they already had jobs waiting for them. In like manner, acts sent from communist countries to perform here invariably contain some performers who choose to stay in America, and who defect while on tour. Their target? Circus Bartok, of course. The staff of the remarkable, doughty one-ringer now includes famed instructors from national schools in Eastern Europe.

In some respects Doc Bartok is like other circus owners. He is on the one hand a hard-headed business man, and on the other, a dreamer. Sitting outside his trailer with him I watched workers go about their chores preparatory for a new season.

"It isn't a show to join if you like sitting on your behind," he said.

Then he paused and pursed his lips, surveying the fifty acres of his winter quarters domain.

"What do you see here? Probably nothing but piles of poles being painted, trailers refurbished,

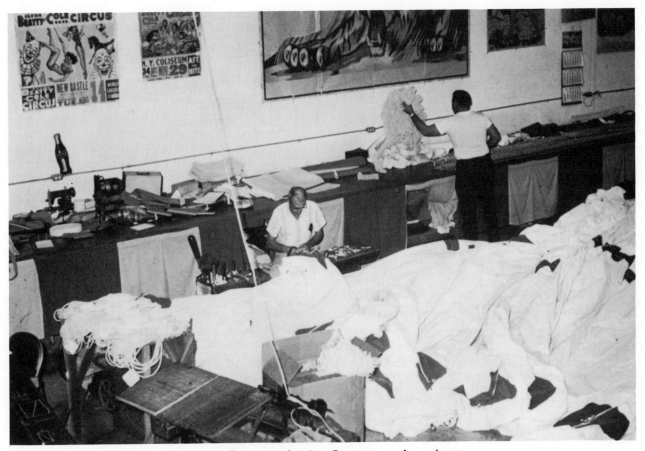

The Leaf Tent and Awning Company, makers of canvas tops for many circuses, works on a new Bartok big top.

discarded trucks and out-of-work animals waiting for a new season to start. But do you know what I see? I see fifty acres of wintertime activity that could serve as a genuine attraction for the county. I see islands of animals, like the one we started this year over there. I see practice rings with arenas and aerial riggings, covered so that we can practice in bad weather. I see color and activity everywhere, and crowds of people waiting to pay admission. Why, we could even train our own performers, and run the place year 'round! It could be the biggest operation the area has ever seen. Why, we could . . . ."

I watched the Florida sunlight glisten and reflect from his glasses. If his image had been furnished with sideburns and jowl-like cheeks he would have resembled a present-day version of the greatest showman America has ever seen.

"If you do not shoot at the sun, you may not hit a star," I said paraphrasing the great Barnum himself.

Doc smiled, recognizing the allusion.

"Perhaps, but maybe it is just a dream," he said quietly.

Perhaps it is. But on the other hand, maybe . . . .

Freshly painted reserved-seat chairs wait in the sun to be loaded for the yearly tour.

Shandra, a Bartok "bull," gets cleaned off prior to her appearance at Sarasota's Hall of Fame.

Alligators, wild on Bartok's winter-quarters property, were simply fenced in and exhibited in their natural habitat.

*Before replacement in 1971, the Bartok generators were
said to have been the oldest on the road.*

*Bunni Bartok-Perz exchanges greetings with a Bartok
lion cub.*

*The modest Grand Entry at Circus Bartok always drew
loud cheers from audiences.*

The Leaf Tent and Awning Company, makers of canvas tops for many circuses, works on a new Bartok big top.

*Zulu, the zebra mare trained by Joyce, gives her handler
a bit of trouble at the early rehearsals.*

*Otto Griebling, the finest pantomime clown yet to appear
in any American circus, was given a tramp suit of silver
tatters for his role in the 100th Anniversary spec.*

Jack Joyce rehearses his Lippizan routine as performed by a pony.

An aerialist spins in the air.

A spellbound audience watches from ringside.

5

A HORSE, A TIGER,
AND A GIRL

"YOU HAVE TO think what you are doing every minute. You have to think what *he* thinks, up there."

The voice was that of the beautiful Evy Althoff, and she spoke of her dangerous, unique, and beautiful routine that combines a Siberian tiger and a horse. The act is devastating, and has had circus audiences on the edge of their seats for years.

The tiger, King by name, was bought when he was three months old by Hans Althoff, who worked the act as his father did, before Evy took it over. At three months King was already a handful, and could never be petted.

"But he had a good character," explained Evy. "You can't touch him or play with him like the tiger in Baumann's act; but if something happens, he has a little rubber mat in the center of the ring and goes to that when anything goes wrong. He feels protected there. Not many tigers would do that. They would fight, or strike out; but they wouldn't go to a little mat like King does. A few days ago the horse—we named him Tiger, of course—got his hind feet tangled in some ropes and we didn't see it. I cued the tiger off the high platform onto the horse's back; and the horse hesitated because of the ropes. The tiger somersaulted in front of the horse and the whole act fell apart. It was a mess. But King went right to the mat and my husband came in and cut the ropes from the horse's feet. I had to pay attention only to King, of course."

The hackles at the back of my neck bristled, and I looked at the lovely girl sitting beside me who had just come matter-of-factly from the ring. It didn't seem possible that such a ladylike girl could possibly undergo such tension twice daily, or that she could have survived an episode like the one she had just described without suffering nervous collapse.

"How did you make up the act to begin with?" I asked.

"It was started when the tiger was very young. What we did was to take the tiger in his little cage inside the big arena cage with the horse. Tiger was the sixth horse that we tried. The others were all scared. Now (did you see it out back?) we have another horse. This is because we must make ready a second in case anything happens. Two years ago, I think it was, the horse saw his reflection in the low glass panels that surround the arena and we couldn't make him work for almost two weeks. It was very difficult.

"The new horse has been in the ring; but he is too young—only about three and a half years old, or so—and we don't want to work him with King yet. But he wasn't scared of the tiger in the portable cage when we had the two in the ring together. Later we tried King on his high, overhead platform; but we didn't make him do anything except to stay there while the new horse went around below. The new horse was OK. So

Seemingly casual, but constantly on the alert, Evy Althoff puts her charges through their paces in the center-ring cage.

was the tiger, but he kept looking down. He knew something was different, but wasn't sure what it was.

"What is the next step?"

"While we are on the road, nothing. In winter quarters last year we got the new horse used to weight on his back."

"How?"

"Hans and I, together with our cousin, Gunther Gebel, all sat on the horse together! Next winter—well, we'll see how far we can go then. But no training on the road. It would be too hard on the tiger. All that jumping up and down all the time is not good for him. Anyhow, tigers are lazy."

I had noticed that Evy often stopped at King's cage and spoke to him before the act began. Afterwards, when the cage was pulled back to the menagerie, I had seen her talking with the animal or stroking it with the butt end of her light cue-whip. Similarly, she often stopped for a few words with the gigantic, spotted horse. During these times, as when she is in the arena, her apparently casual attitude belies her total concentration on her magnificent co-stars. All three are so attuned to one another that their appearance seems like that of a single entity in three phases. Their communication is so remarkable that if one falters the others automatically adjust.

Such extraordinary, inter-specific communication gives the illusion of ease and informality. But it is actually a case where each participant is geared at concert pitch. The limits of understanding (even on Evy's part) and communication are pushed so far, and the attunement is so tight that the act is surely one of the most dangerous in the circus world today. It would not be going too far to say that because of Evy Althoff it is also one of the most beautiful.

6

SUPERSTAR

IN 1969 CIRCUS audiences were stunned by the debut of a trainer so charismatic, so appealing, and so talented that they could hardly believe their eyes. Ringling Bros. Circus had brought to America a young man named Gunther Gebel-Williams, a trainer that appeared with his own herd of elephants, a troupe of horses, and a collection of Bengal tigers.

In one of his acts Williams mixed an Indian and African elephant together with a Bengal tiger. Finally allowing the Indian elephant to leave the arena, he then cued the tiger onto the robed back of the remaining elephant and dashed quickly up a ladder over the elephant's rump to sit cockily astride the Bengal, as the elephant saluted with its trunk, and slowly revolved on its pedestal.

Gebel-Williams is one of those magical personalities who exerts as much influence on his audience as he does on the animals he trains. His presence is instantly felt by everyone within range. It is a positive feeling, as if everyone who sees him is working *for* him, either mentally, as in the case of the audiences, or physically, as in the case of the animals. This is important if he is to be a success before audiences, certainly; and it is this quality that makes him the leading trainer of the day.

Nowhere is this rapport more evident than when he is in the ring with his tigers, and nowhere is the poetry of his technique more obvious and pleasing to see. (He knows this, of course, and gives his appearances a little extra "oomph" to accentuate the pleasure afforded his audience.)

Blessed with the shape of a sapling willow and a shock of silver-blonde hair, Williams enters the arena cage scantily dressed. He wears boots, spangled tights to his waist and a brief, network bolero. Sometimes he wears a gaudy cross. Some spectators have accused him of promoting a sexual image, citing his customary ring costume as proof of this fact, but this assessment is more indicative of the spectator's attitudes than of Williams's approach to his art.

Williams, it should be emphasized, is an extremely open personality (as, indeed, are many superstars). He is a natural man, aware of his own attractiveness and reveling in it. The purpose behind the costumes he wears is only partly one of attraction. Importantly, his close-fitting costume guarantees him maximum freedom from snags against the equipment that he must heave around. He feels unencumbered, in this manner, and seems to transmit the idea that he, too, is an animal; and that his motions are as much to be admired as are those of his tigers. He is correct.

The walkaround is a case in point. Williams stands in the center of the ring, and cues his tigers to line up side by side, abreast of him so that they extend like a single spoke in a wheel to the edge of the arena. The eye of every tiger is upon him as he pivots slowly with his arms extended. The entire file of tigers moves in unison around him, each animal constantly checking the actions of its trainer with furtive glances while snarling protests to its neighbor, lest it get out of line. Those that fall behind receive a reminder from a long whip, and scurry back into place. The whole motion is fluid, as the sinewy, striped, animal bodies automatically reveal the control that keeps their pent-up energies in check. Williams, dead sure of himself, appears at once acutely in tune with the wheel of savagery that turns around his legs and, at the same time, utterly relaxed. He talks constantly to the cats, calling each by name if he suspects insubordination. When a momentary argument breaks out between cats, it lasts less than a second or two, for a crack from the Williams whip is over the scene instantly, reminding the tigers that Big Brother is watching—*always.*

The Williams biography is an interesting one. The superstar was born in 1936 as Gunther Gebel in Schweidnitz, a city that was ceded to Poland after World War II. While still a youth, young Gunther and his mother fled advancing Russian armies until they reached Cologne, where they subsisted as best they could until Mrs. Gebel located work as a seamstress with Circus Williams, which was based in that city.

Mrs. Gebel didn't remain with the circus, but Mr. Williams, its director, became fond of young Gunther and adopted him. Gebel-Williams took to the circus arts brilliantly, and showed such a leaning towards association with animals that his stepfather guided him into work as a trainer. As soon as Gunther mastered one type of animal he was introduced to another, until he had run the gamut from horses to lions, to elephants, and, finally, to tigers.

Several years later Mr. Williams was killed during a circus chariot race. A year after that Williams's true son, Gebel—Williams's stepbrother, died as well. So at the age of sixteen Gebel-Williams found himself the kingpin of a famous circus. With the widow Williams managing the business end of the show, Gunther emerged as the boss of backstage teardowns and the feature of the performance as well.

He married Jeanette Williams, a featured equestrienne with the circus and his stepsister, but later divorced her and married Sigrid, his current wife. (Sigrid, like Gebel-Williams himself, was not born into the circus tradition. She was merely a star-struck spectator who managed to attract Gebel-Williams's attention when she sat ringside.)

Gebel-Williams has emerged from this complex, fairy-tale-like background as the *sine qua non* of trainers in the 1970s. His tiger performance on Ringling's Red Unit is fantastically beautiful and altogether unique, *and* he presents a brilliant elephant act as well, *and* he supervises his wife and former wife during their presentations of liberty horse routines. Formerly he rode in an opening display of Roman post riding (standing, with one foot astride each of two horses) but has now delegated this to an assistant.

Animals are his world, and he has little time or inclination for anything else. He even slept with his star tiger when he first purchased it at six months of age. The togetherness that developed between the man and his feline allowed the creation of Williams's feature act—the pyramid of elephant, tiger, and Gebel-Williams himself, as top mounter.

A person of great exactitude, Williams expects the same from his grooms and workers. He rarely speaks with strangers. In 1971 I visited the backstage area of the Ringling show at least twice weekly for seven weeks. I saw Williams constantly, and often passed him no more than two feet away; but never once did his gaze extend in my direction. One simply didn't say hello on a casual basis and expect to receive an answer from a man as dedicated and preoccupied.

It was not until 1973 that I was able to arrange an interview with Williams, and discover that the awe in which he is held by "towners" like myself had gone too far in eclipsing the warmth and humor that exists in the personality of the great trainer. Although he expects results when he deals with both people and animals, he is positive and pleasant, rather than stiff and demanding in his approach.

But who can deny Gebel-Williams's talent, or his electric appeal to the circus audience? The man is fantastic; there is no getting around it. He has brought new life to the American circus scene, and has taken his place among those in the very top drawer of animal training all over the world. He is, as many have claimed, the standard by which most other trainers will be judged in the future. His acts, while lacking the nobility and beauty of Alfred Court's in the 1940s, are the best seen in a quarter of a century. They will always be remembered. Although the circus sells Gebel-Williams partly as a personality, time will bend the sapling willow, and will leave the audience's memory focussed where it should be—on his accomplishments.

Indeed, accomplishments are Williams's specialties. Proof of the fact was his development of the tiger-elephant-trainer pyramid for Ringling Bros.' 1973 edition of its Red Unit. In a climactic feature, the trainer mixed two horses, his African elephant and no less than three tigers in the ring at the same time. Not content with this feat, he rode astride his tiger atop an African elephant around the hippodrome track, completely free and uncaged. The display was convincing proof that Williams is as close to an absolute master of wild animals as we are likely to see.

The old circus philosophy still holds true. It's not what you *are*, in a circus, but what you *do*, that counts.

Gebel-Williams

At a cue from Gebel-Williams, a group of tigers advances to the proper position.

*With Gebel-Williams as its central anchor, a file of
tigers revolves around the ring like a spoke in a wheel.*

*Tiger and trainer drop simultaneously from a standing
position, forming a final pose.*

A tableau from the Gebel-Williams elephant act.

The pièce de résistance of all Gebel-Williams's training. African elephant, Bengal tiger, and superstar pile atop one another.

The lifeblood of any performer is applause. Gebel-Williams accepts his, which is usually thunderous, with consummate style.

The lithe form of Gebel-Williams seems utterly relaxed as he lands on an elephant's back. Moments before this photo was taken, he was catapulted through the air from a teeterboard that was slammed to the ground by a second elephant.

Gebel-Williams is dwarfed by the largest tiger in his act's opening tableau. (Photo by permission of Ringling Bros. Circus, courtesy of Solters, Sabinson and Raskin)

In a stunt called the walkaround, Gebel-Williams acts as a pivot point for a line of snarling tigers. (Photo by permission of Ringling Bros. Circus, courtesy Solters, Sabinson and Raskin)

Gebel-Williams poses assuredly next to a sea of tiger stripes (Photo by permission of Ringling Bros. Circus, courtesy of Solters, Sabinson and Raskin)

Dressed gladiator style, Gebel-Williams faces one of his big cats. (Photo by permission of Ringling Bros. Circus, courtesy Solters, Sabinson and Raskin)

Gebel-Williams with two of his horse-riding tigers. (Photo by permission of Ringling Bros. Circus, courtesy of Solters, Sabinson and Raskin)

Like father, like son . . . young Oliver is introduced to life in the ring by his gifted father. (Photo by permission of Ringling Bros. Circus, courtesy of Solters, Sabinson and Raskin)

Strictly for publicity, Gebel-Williams strikes a pose for the press. (Photo by permission of Ringling Bros. Circus, courtesy of Solters, Sabinson and Raskin)

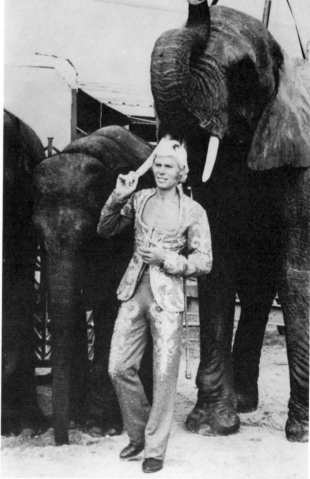

Gunther and his beautiful wife Sigrid strike an exultant pose during the elephant act. (Photo by permission of Ringling Bros. Circus, courtesy of Solters, Sabinson and Raskin)

Off-beat attire seems to go well with tigers as Gunther poses with a feline friend during rehearsals in Venice, Florida. (Photo by permission of Ringling Bros. Circus, courtesy of Solters, Sabinson and Raskin)

Williams poses in front of his female African elephant— one of the few performing in the ring. (Photo by permission of Ringling Bros. Circus, courtesy Solters, Sabinson and Raskin)

7

FOUR-FOOTED FRENZY

IF ONE TALKS about circus dogs these days, one talks about the Stephensons. This remarkable family from Portrush, Northern Ireland, made its debut with Ringling Bros. Circus in New York City in 1959. Not only do its members train and present dogs brilliantly, but they also present a fast-paced riding act, billed as the riding Saxons. In the 100th Anniversary production of Ringling Bros. Circus Mrs. Stephenson made two appearances in the ring. Flo, the elder sister, made six appearances, and her younger sister made five. Three male Stephensons completed the roster of six.

Strictly center-ring material, the Stephensons are far outnumbered by their dogs. The total number of canines touring with the Stephensons in 1970 was a staggering thirty-five. The majority were registered purebred wire-haired and smooth-haired terriers. A stunning complement of apricot poodles is featured, together with larger, show poodles—each doing his particular specialty. Three mutts have the honor of appearing with this prestigious act. Their names are Judy, Frisky, and Kevin.

Among the favorite routines that the Stephenson dogs perform are two that are world famous. One is a high jump into a sheet (held by Mrs. Stephenson and Flo) by a terrier that appears to know no fear. No hesitation is apparent as the dog scampers his way to the top of a high ladder and plunges into the "safety net" sheet. His tail wags all the way! The other routine is the frenzied and rousing finale, with terriers dashing everywhere around the ring curb, jumping over still more ter-

riers who run in the opposite direction wearing little hurdles on their backs. It is a finale that has yet to be equalled in circusdom, and has made many a spectator aware of dog acts for the first time. Zest, humor, and high style are the ingredients that make the canine *tour de force* the most exciting and best of its kind anywhere today.

Although thirty-five dogs are owned by the Stephensons, thirty constitute the full-performing complement. They are tethered backstage, are brought out to "do their thing" and returned to their backstage post. The canines are placed at their "ready stations" thirty minutes before the act goes on because it takes that length of time to get such a quantity of animals situated in the right order, groomed, and otherwise prepared for their appearance. Three ponies are used in the act as well. All of these animals travel overland in two trucks, while the Stephensons themselves travel in cars that pull two large house trailers. Their heavy-ring horses, used in their bareback riding act, travel by train.

The Stephensons also support a fluctuating number of transient, canine guests that are sent to them by people who sense the great rapport between the Stephensons and all dogs. Most of these are ailing, and are nursed back to health by the Stephensons, then presented to friends along the circus route. Two members of the circus troupe that do not appear in the ring are in training. Three "retired" dogs also travel with the family simply because the Stephensons cannot bear to part with them. One of these is a remarkable and much-loved dog that reached its twenty-second year in 1970. This ancient performer sees and hears perfectly—testament to the Stephensons' excellent care of their animals. Its hindquarters are weakening, but it eats well, and will be kept as long as it lives.

An interview with the Stephensons is best conducted at a shout, because the dogs tethered outside the trailer continually bark at the presence of a "foreigner." But the bounce and excitement of the dogs are highly contagious. They are obviously happy, and carry their joyous élan with them into the ring. Each is desperately fond of Mrs. Stephenson in particular, and dotes on her approval. They usually get it in the form of an exuberant bear hug, as they leap into her arms in the ring.

If there is one quality that makes this remarkable act succeed, it is not the training (which is of a very high order) or the style of presentation (which is also brilliant). It is the unabashed joy, happiness, and pleasure—not to mention the excitement—with which these incredible canines zoom through their routines. Every face in the bleachers smiles at the Stephensons' dogs. The wild applause that the act receives is richly deserved. Purebred or mutt, the performers are winners all.

In 1972, Flo Stephenson talked with me during a break between performances, in order to tell me a little about training and to inform me of a four-footed, New York debut.

"Pepe is new this year, but perhaps you didn't notice, since he replaces a dog that looked just like him. He is a silver miniature poodle. His act is quite complicated for a little fellow, and he hasn't settled into it fully yet."

I remembered a silver poodle that ran across the ring on its hind legs and left by opening and closing a little gate. I asked Flo if that was the dog she described.

"Yes, except that Pepe does much more. The trick is really one of a series of tricks. First he sits up on top of my head while I stand on my sister's shoulders—we call that the three-high. Then we break and seemingly all tumble to the ground and do a rollover, except that Pepe is put upon the ground. If he jumped he might hurt himself by landing incorrectly. After that we perform what is termed jumps 'n' rolls. It's the same thing you see three gymnasts doing on mats, but Pepe takes the place of a third person. It's only after all of that, that he walks across the arena

on his own and opens the little gate. After he goes through it, he closes it and then jumps into Mama's (Lucy Stephenson's) arms, and the routine is over. It's quite a lot for a little dog to remember. Besides, when he is on top of my head he can see what's going on in the other two rings; and he doesn't pay enough attention to his work at that point. That's when I am trying to push his front feet up, and my voice is very nasty and hateful, even though I am smiling for the sake of the audience. The others down below are all telling me whether Pepe is doing what he's supposed to or not. Billy or Mama is usually yelling, 'He's not up yet—not yet!' but the audience can't hear it because of the band and the confusion, of course."

"For a new performer, he seems to be doing very well," I offered. "When did you get him?"

"Just a year ago, right here in New York City. We carried him on the road, rehearsing two or three times a week, until he got the hang of it. He became a full-fledged performer in Venice, Florida, in January, 1972."

"What are the first things that you taught him?"

"To sit up. That's always first, although we don't consider that a trick really. It's part of general discipline. After that we taught him the roll over. That's very hard, because he rolls over on either side, depending on the cue he's given."

"How did you go about it? Is that a trade secret?"

"No it isn't; but Billy did most of the training. You pull his head to the ground gently but firmly until he goes down onto one shoulder. When his hind end starts to follow, you push him into a rollover, saying, 'Roll!' at the same time. Of course, once you get him back on his feet you make a big fuss over him, and compliment him, and pat him, so that he wants to earn the same affection when you try it the next time. With a dog as smart as Pepe, learning a trick like that doesn't take long."

"How did you train your high-diving dog to jump into the sheet?"

"Oh, that's Spot. He's a terrier, and terriers love to climb and jump. We've got quite a few out back that climb right up the wire fencing and jump out of their kennels! Getting him to jump isn't hard when you've got Mama waiting down below. Spot is wild about Mama. He is so excited climbing the ladder that he sometimes falls off it backwards. That's why Dinah is below. It happened three times recently, and scared us to death. It didn't scare Spot at all, naturally—just us."

"I don't know whether we invented the high-diving dog trick or not; but we've always had one. My grandfather had one in his own act back in Ireland, and that was seventy or eighty years ago. Once we had a greyhound that did it. We were touring in Germany, and he jumped right off a bridge for the sheer joy of it. The Rhine was below—fortunately."

"Does Spot also take part in the race around the ring curb?"

"Of course. He loves it. He was the one that got so excited the other night that he fell off. Dinah picked him up, gave him a whack on the behind, and he was off and away again. But Kevin —he was our star jumper in the runaround finale. He really threw himself into the trick, and usually brought the house down with applause."

"He isn't doing it anymore?"

"Kevin has retired from the runaround. I'm sure he would be embarrassed if he knew I told you, but Kevin got too middle-aged for all that jumping. It happens to all of us, you know."

"All of you?" I grinned at Flo as I was about to answer her; but she caught my intent and finished the subject herself.

"All of us except for Mama," she said. "She's the only one who never tires in the ring. The Stephensons are the Stephensons because of her; and that goes for all the people, all the dogs, and all the horses in our riding act, too!"

Flo was right. I learned this as I watched Stephenson's Dogs a short while later. The training may have been largely Billy's, and the human participants may have been supporting family members, but the pace, style, and warmth emanated from the senior member of the troupe—Lucy Stephenson. Petite, with her dark hair strikingly and plainly styled, and with more bounce to her step than is displayed by a dozen teenagers, she is outgoing in her manner of performance—breezy and joyous—the embodiment of the spirit of the circus.

8

THE CONVICTS

I AM TEMPTED to believe that zebras seem to be among the most highly individualistic mammals as far as temperament is concerned, for conflicting opinions seem to be the rule concerning the docility of these beasts. In captivity, especially in zoos, they have been known to prefer the hand that feeds them to the food it holds. One authority claims that zebra stallions "and even an occasional mare" can be violently aggressive, dangerous animals, that do not hesitate to attack a human. But he counters this information with the fact that two stallions in his zoo's collection appear to be calm and docile. Apparently not satisfied with this generous statement, he then claims that "no keeper would risk a real test." That is how it seems to be with zebras. Nobody dares to commit himself in the psychological department, at least no one prominent in the zoological profession. It may be that authorities have done some work towards unravelling this interesting facet of the zebra history, but it is buried in the technical literature, not easily available to the merely curious.

Perhaps, after all, zoological authorities are too erudite to see the simple facts. Feeling that this might be the case, I eagerly accepted an invitation from Jack Joyce, former performance director of Ringling Bros. Circus, as he was about to "break" a new act consisting of two llamas, three shetland ponies, a Sicilian donkey, and a zebra for Circus Bartok. The zebra, owned by Mr. Joyce, is a member of the mountain zebra species, with heavy markings to the hoofs and the characteristic gridiron along its spine. There

was no mistaking the Sandler ranch, outside of Venice, Florida, where Jack was training. There simply wasn't another "striped horse" grazing in any other ranch along the roadside.

I made the trip accompanied by my friend and photographic mentor, Slim Sommers. Equipped with far too much paraphernalia for comfort in the murderous humidity of Florida, we leaned on the fence rail gazing at the impressively handsome animal as it munched grasses. Slim, an ex-rodeo hand who had specialized in riding Brahmas, looked the mare over in a professional manner, then turned to me and said "Whaddayaknowbout zebras?"

"Nothing," I quickly answered. Then, after a pause, I amended the statement, adding, "Nothing good, that is."

Slim snorted, opened the gate and walked up to the mare. Without hesitation he gave her shoulder a healthy pat, an action that brought the zebra's head up, so that she could more easily nuzzle a kindred spirit.

I thought I heard him mumble something about "authors with too much book learnin'" and couldn't have agreed with him more as I hurried into the corral to examine the animal more closely.

My general feelings about animals were all corroborated in my subsequent investigation of that beautiful beast. To learn about an animal one does not (as Slim would be quick to agree) read a book, theorize, make conjectures, analyze anatomy, or study diet charts. All of these have their place in the appreciation and understanding of an animal but a beast is not what we say it is, or think it is, or hear it is. It is what it is, and must be understood and appreciated from its own point of view. It must be seen, heard, felt, and smelled before we really know what it is all about. The animal that is in us understands instinctively what our brains can never explain.

The mare was vividly patterned, stocky, and altogether lovable. The tang of her odor dilated our nostrils, the velvet touch of her lips played gently on our palms as we offered her grass that we tore from the ground, and the brilliance and tightness of her close-cropped fur, so finely delineated that it seemed almost painted onto her hide, amazed us. Between Slim, myself, and the exotic and beautiful animal before us no tension existed. It was one of those rare moments when nature combined three existences for a fraction of a second, and everything was right with the world.

"Oh. You and Zulu get along, I see."

It was the voice of Jack Joyce, just arrived in the corral to begin training. We smiled a greeting, and noticed that a small group of interested visitors had assembled for the lesson and had been watching, a bit awed, at our association with the zebra.

Joyce explained that not only the zebra but the ponies, llamas, and Sicilian donkey, all assembled for rehearsal, were equally calm and approachable by anyone. He told us that the routine about to be practiced was one that the animals had known several years before, but would have to learn again, after having performed a different routine since.

The zebra was sent into the ring, a circular construction with high, slatted walls that eliminated the possibility of an animal leaping over the curb. She was trotted around at a casual pace by Joyce, who kept up a running commentary in a low voice from the center. Sometimes he would raise his voice slightly, but it was always to speak with the spectators, never to the zebra. Zulu's commands were given in a low-key, relaxed tone, and seemed to exude patience. No excitement was apparent (and, in fact, none existed) as the perky animal bounced and trotted around the ring. Many times she missed her cue, and had to be sent back for another try. Her confusion was apparent from the sound of her high-pitched whinny-whistle, a sound unlike that made by any other member of the horse family.

Never did Joyce raise his voice. Never did he ply her with either of his two long whips, except to tickle her rump when she needed a reminder.

"The whips are really only an extension of your arms," he said in an explanation that was unnecessary.

Slim joined me at ringside and whispered into my ear, "I wish to God those old fuddy-duddies that complain to the SPCA could see *this!*"

Again, he was right. It was quickly apparent that the temperament of Zulu was directly related to the temperament of her talented coach. I thought about this as I watched the remarkable demonstration. Perhaps the ugliness and volatile nature of zebras, recounted in so many zoological texts, resulted from the treatment they had received prior to their incarceration in zoo stalls. Perhaps the caution, not to say the fear, demonstrated by zookeepers new to the animals, merely represented an extension of that same frame of mind that brought the zebras into captivity in the first place. The training period continued.

"The famous Lippizan stallions of Vienna jump because they are strictly schooled to do so," Joyce continued, "but the 'airs above ground,' in which the horse jumps from all four feet into the air, then kicks out while airborne, existed long before that. Zebras knew all about it for years, because they were always preyed upon, and needed every defense to overcome their adversaries."

A tickle from the whip and Zulu flew into the air, extended her legs and presented such a vicious kick with her hind legs that the sound of her hoofs striking accidentally together could easily be heard at the next ranch, half a mile down the road.

The visiting audience gasped. Several women placed their hands protectively on their bosoms. Slim and I grinned at each other, for we knew and appreciated nature in the raw, and were amused at the ladies' amazement and apprehension at its violence and force.

Uncontrollably, my voice sounded a parody of the circus chord that finished a completed feat in the ring.

"Ta-Daaaaaaaa!"

The tourists broke into relieved laughter at what they considered my drollery. But Slim didn't, nor did Jack Joyce, nor John, his stablemaster. All of us knew that the rhythm and pace and choreography of that moment called for such a sound, that it was not an artificial embellishment, created to add an effect. It was an emotionally prompted, humanization of a telling, natural moment, and we all recognized it accordingly.

Zulu completed her routine, making many mistakes as she did so. But Joyce did not attempt to

Zulu, the zebra mare trained by Joyce, gives her handler a bit of some trouble at the early rehearsals.

Jack Joyce's zebra, Zulu.

force her, to reprimand her unduly, or to become insistent about her failures. Time was the answer to her troubles. Brilliant trainer of hoofed stock that he is, Joyce had long ago programmed the zebra's progress so that she was progressing exactly according to his plan, no matter how casual it appeared.

Following rehearsal in the ring, Zulu was allowed her freedom among the spectators. For the most part she ignored them, preferring to munch grass and relax. But a few "clucks" from Slim brought her to us, and she calmly nuzzled us again as we fed her bits of carrot.

At that time (and even now) I was almost willing to return home and throw every textbook out with the trash. My twelve years experience with animals, nine of them under the professional tutelage of zoological park authorities, were as nothing compared to the hour's time spent in the presence of the remarkable trainer, Jack Joyce.

At last I knew what a zebra was all about.

9

HIGH OVER THE CENTER RING

ROBBED OF LIGHT, save for the sterile grays of low-wattage work lamps, the circus arena takes on a cold atmosphere. Color and confusion have been snuffed out. Even midway during the performance, such sudden deadening of sight and sound have a peculiar effect. From somewhere the hum of a generator is heard. Distant voices shout orders, and the metallic clank of heavy apparatus is heard as it is shunted into place amidst the gloom. Shadowy forms trot about the arena, performing their chores regardless of the blackness.

It is an unusual moment, but one that occurs, now and then, in every circus. Timing has gone off, if even for a minute or two, and promoted an instant of singular effect. But the moment is short-lived.

As suddenly as conditions fall apart they mesh again. The performing artists, the announcer, the band, and the crew that mans the spotlights all snap into action, and the leviathan of a show lifts again to life.

A pernicious roll snaps from the snare drum at the very moment when a single spotlight beam cuts the blackness of the arena's dome. The light catches three lithe and handsome forms perched on a tiny platform high in the air. A *diminuendo* on the drum. The announcer's voice begins that magical phrase, "High over the center ring . . ."

For thousands of circus fans the world over the ultimate moment has arrived. The flyers are about to "make their turn."

Flying is a very special art. Those who specialize in the flying trapeze are, indeed, very special people. Accused of a certain *hauteur* by other members of the performing complement that makes up a circus, their so-called snobbishness is in reality nothing more than total concentration on their own sphere of activity. Theirs is a sophisticated art, requiring rigorous training and powers of concentration that are kept well honed for every moment of their act (in this respect they match cat trainers). Furthermore, trapeze artists who work "catch acts" have a relatively short performing career; flying is an art that requires appearance. Figures must look well when flying through the air. Paunches, saggy thighs, or knees that look like knobs are not permissible over the center ring. An exception to this harsh aesthetic ruling is sometimes the catcher, who is the real workhorse of a catch act. Because he is not the star from the audience's point of view, and because his role is less showy than that of the artists who seem to flip so casually through the air, he is allowed a certain degree of heftiness and maturity. From the point of view of the flyers themselves, there is another reason for allowing a less glamorous physique to maintain the catcher's post. He must be strong, and he must be reliable. These requisites come before appearance where catchers are concerned. No matter how perfectly a flyer can perform a double somersault, he will fail if the catcher is not there to grasp his wrists instantaneously, at precisely the correct moment.

Flyers make contact by slapping their hands around each other's wrists—not by catching hands. The reason for this is that the enormous pull of gravity at the lowest point of the swing is severe enough to tear ordinary handholds apart. By grabbing wrists, the downward pull acts as a strength-ening force as each hand slides down the arm of the other flyer, to be made firm against the heel of his hand. Properly executed, the moment of contact is a thing of great beauty and, without the music that plays during an actual performance, the slap of hands on wrists echoes throughout the whole arena. It is a sound that makes other flyers, on the ground below, smile knowingly; they understand at once that a good catch has been made, even without looking up.

If one talks about flyers, one talks about Antoinette Concello and that is that. She and her husband, Arthur, both stopped flying in 1943; but she is still to be seen on the floor of the arena, watching the famed Ringling aerial ballet like a hawk. Since her flying days she has become Ringling's aerial director, and it has been her supervision that has tightened and sparked that theatrical chromo over the years. But her greatest feat in circusdom was the mastering of that ultimate flyer's goal, the triple. Art Concello had been performing it regularly after the Concellos took over the center ring following a lay-up by the fabulous Alfredo Codona back in the old days. It was he who finally said to her, in his matter-of-fact manner, that it was time to try the triple; an announcement that, Antoinette recalls, scared her silly. She did it, and soon performed it regularly with him over the center ring. Such a duo has never been equalled since. Starting in 1969, two triples have been performed, one over each end ring. The Gaonas perform one, and the Flying Waynes take care of the other. As thrilling as it is, it cannot compare with the other, since both are performed by males. Only in the 1930s did the "Big One" boast a triple performed by a woman—with her husband performing it just before. It was clearly a plethora of excellence, the sort of incomparability for which Ringling has been famous at certain times. And no one did it with more style than "Tony." Her form was flawless. She seemed to be almost inhuman in her perfection.

But Antoinette Concello was not inhuman. She was *more* than human. She was one of those remarkable individuals who could perform her grueling turn on the trapeze and make it seem almost casual. If she was concerned about her performance, no one knew it. Richly deserving her publicized title "Queen of the Flying Trapeze," everything she did was professional. Sure of herself as a person and absolutely confident of her

technique, she was a winner all the way.

In the 1970s, as she stands beneath the aerial ballet girls on their single strand webs, you can tell that she is still a pro. She knows what she is doing—and every girl aloft is in there pitching because of Tony.

In my estimation, there is only one point in Ringling aerial ballet that is truly effective: the violent spinning of the girls at the conclusion of their aerial display. The mass effect here is stunning, and has remained so over the years. The rest seems pretty but unexceptional. Its main interest is in its timing, and it remains an amazement to me that so many girls can be engineered through such a welter of ups, downs, ins, and outs and still end up all together.

Yet in the middle of this pulchritudinous excess there exists a "star" or stars over the center ring. This central attraction is used as a focal point, around which the dizzying damsels cavort, turning themselves into a setting for what is supposed to be the Ringling crown jewel of the season. Often the jewel is not as important as its setting; the surrounding hoopla has, on occasion, surpassed the feature. But there have been a few genuine attractions used as aerial ballet features. You can tell when a real one comes along, for the star usually lasts more than two seasons.

There was one such center-ring attraction more famous than any other. Her name was Leitzel, of course, and hers was a far earlier day than mine, but the legend of her one arm planges (giant swings of the entire body, around one arm that grasps a single rope) is famous. Later artists (Lalage and, more recently, LaToria) have duplicated her routine, but never equalled it. Leitzel apparently had that magic something that sold her to her audiences. She was a true superstar.

Years ago there appeared a diminutive girl with a unique center-ring turn. Appearing barefoot, she was pulled to her single trapeze over the center ring. There she swung back and forth while standing on the trapeze without holding on with her hands. She stopped the swing; then swung sideways. During this routine she faced the end rings, after which she repeated this routine kneeling, with one leg extended backwards in the air. Next she sat on a chair, two legs of which rested on the trapeze bar, and swung back and forth. Finally she swung the trapeze at breakneck speed in a huge circle. She stood on her toes on the bar, teetering frantically back and forth, on the very

Pinito del Oro. (Courtesy Circus World Museum, Bara-boo, Wisconsin)

brink of death at each turn. The entire, amazing routine was performed barefoot, without holding on with her hands—and without a net. Her husband stood below. The name of this fantastic star was Pinito del Oro (translated by the circus management as "Little Pine Tree of Gold"). For many years she graced the center ring and gave the life of consummate skill to her routine. The act brought the entire aerial ballet to life, and was eagerly awaited by the audience.

Did I say that her skill was consummate? It was, but not always. Suddenly, one year, there was no Pinito del Oro to catch the breath of audiences all over America. She had fallen and seriously injured herself during a winter engagement in Europe. She has never been replaced, even though acts of great expertise have been

seen in that precious, center-ring spotlight. Magnificently performed heel catches, executed by "the electric Elvin Bale" with brilliant showmanship, certainly equal the awesome gyrations of Pinito del Oro in their way; but still they do not strike the chord, or engender a response similar to that brought forth by the Little Pine Tree of Gold, or her legendary predecessor, Lillian Leitzel.

Perhaps what American audiences need is a brilliant aerial star who is also diminutive. Perhaps the tiny dimensions of a single, female star, holding all eyes upon her, engender a sympathy that accompanies our amazement at the brilliance of her performance.

The spot is waiting for its future legend, a single, focal point of brilliance begging to be filled in the most magnificent circus on earth.

10

LIONMASTERS

"I DON'T TALK so good English." The voice was that of the burly Wolfgang Holzmair, trainer of the largest group of lions presented anywhere today. Seventeen cats perform, and all but one are females. Holzmair uses only one male because he finds that two fight each other, causing tension among the female witnesses and otherwise riling up the act. Avoidance of this seems reasonable when you see the cats in action, for it is one of the most active, fast-paced, and rousing lion acts seen since the heyday of Clyde Beatty.

The performance consists mostly of running leaps across a space between two high stools. Other stools are placed so that they lead up to the jumping-off point. The lionesses leap frantically from each side to the other, performing their jumps quickly, noisily, and alternately, so that the impression is of lions popping in quick succession across the chasm, first from the right and then from the left. They leap first through a metal hoop, next through a whip that is held over the trainer's head, and, finally, with magenta floodlights plunging the arena into lurid eeriness, through a flaming hoop held aloft by Holzmair. During all this time the circus band is screaming at such volume, and the lions are roaring and striking out with such wild (if mock) fury, that the total effect is one of utter panic. It is a genuine thriller and pure circus.

Scratching his right sideburn (that concealed a stitched-up scar from an injury he received earlier during the season) Holzmair struggled to remember how many years he had been training animals, and to say it in English.

"You mean dis vun? Mit de lions? Oder mit dé lions und tigers. Jah, dat was from zwelf years mit de lions und tigers. I do de lions now two years. Aber before all dat I vorked tsen years mit horses und elephants, und chimps, too. This is de first year I do only one act here mit Ringling."

He corrected himself to say that he had performed the lion act four years, but only two of them with Ringling Bros. Circus. Prior to that the act had been with France's famous Cirque Amar, where Holzmair had made his home for twelve years.

All the lions are approximately the same age, a fact that Holzmair considers pertinent to the success of the act. He prefers lions at fifteen to eighteen months as new pupils ("lions den is no baby, is no man") because they are old enough to concentrate on learning, without becoming distracted easily or tiring quickly, as do smaller cubs. Fifteen months places lions closer to teenage delinquency than full maturity, so that plenty of excess energy can be applied to their fast-paced routines.

I remembered that Gunther Gebel-Williams had been quoted in a press release as saying that he preferred tigers to lions for training purposes. (His status as a superstar and elephant and tiger trainer in no way eclipses the flamboyant talents of Wolfgang Holzmair, incidentally.) The impression I received was that Williams felt lions to be more sneaky, an opinion I mentioned to Holzmair.

This brought confused reactions not only from the trainer, but also from his wife, who had been sitting at the rear of the dressing room tossing

Holzmair shifts the enormous weight of a full-grown lion onto his shoulders.

words into the conversation from time to time in an effort to help her husband express himself. She appeared startled, and began a riotous pantomime of a tiger stalking, fingernails extended, followed by a lion attacking. Together, the two of them finally settled on the definition of a tiger acting like a typical cat, and a lion somehow approaching the technique of a dog when it attacks. Holzmair, amused, finally broke through his language barrier and settled the problem once and for all by stating emphatically and in perfect English, "With the lion, when he comes he comes. You kill—you kill, and that is that!"

During the first year that Holzmair's lions gave birth, fourteen or fifteen cubs were born, but all were killed. This is not unusual among wild cats, especially if they live in cramped quarters. The first birth is often swiftly followed by infanticide. Currently there are several cubs, all nursing and progressing well. Holzmair dislikes the small travel cages in which the lions live, and attempts to counteract the confinement as best he can by leaving doors open between hitched cages, so that the animals can walk the length of four or five dens if they desire.

Because of this lack of space Holzmair feeds his lions as much as they can eat without becoming obese and lethargic.

Lazy they are not, as they dash about the large ring. But Holzmair was quick to point out that each lion has its seat, and never gets down from it unless cued to do so.

"You see, de lions have much respect, und so do I," he said, scratching his scar again. "I turn my back all de time. I no have to see what's going on behind me. If the lion move, I feel it. I know." He touched his brow.

"Back to that scar you keep touching," I said. "When did that happen—I mean, at what point in the act?"

"Well, you know in de very end, when all de lions except one is out." (They dash madly between Holzmair's legs into the chutes.) "Dere is dat big lioness what I carry on my shoulders to de chutes. She is de one. But she no try to kill me. She is weigh three hundret twenty—three hundret fifty pounts. When she move on my shoulders, dat's too much. I go down mit her. If she stays, unt doesn't moof, dat's allright. I can make it. But when she moofs, she bring her back foot up to jump off, and she scratch me. It happen in Baltimore a little while ago, too."

Holzmair glanced at his watch, indicating, I thought, the approach of performance time. Taking my cue, I switched the tape recorder off and unthinkingly mumbled *"Bien, c'est assez. Merci."* Both the trainer and his wife broke into laughter. Frau Holzmair pointed at me, laughing, and said *"Vous, vous parlez français mon ami?* But so do vee! It vould haff been so much easier!"

I left them with their illusions about my linguistic abilities, wandered to ringside where the show had already begun, and felt that old tingle of anticipation as the announcer's voice echoed through the arena.

"From France's famous Circus Amar we proudly present Wolfgang Holzmair, the King of the Lions!"

TA DAAAAAAAAAAAAAAAAAAAAAAAA!
It was no understatement.

Hail, Conquering Hero Holzmair!

Right on target—Holzmair style.

At the same time that Holzmair had his lions well in hand on Ringling's Red Unit, the ten-lion display on the same circus's Blue Unit was beautifully presented by a chunky Spaniard, Pablo Noël.

New to the United States, where he made his Ringling debut in 1972, Noël made a sensational impression on American audiences not for what his lions did, but because of what he did with them.

His act consisted of a few tableaux, in which pyramids of lions were formed on various pedestals—but these were the easy tricks. As soon as the felines were in the arena, Noël approached a large male, yanked its jaws open and thrust his head completely into the beast's mouth. So well ensconced was the hapless trainer's skull in those massive jaws, that the lion's impressive canines caressed the back of Noël's head and neck. As if to make matters even more dangerous, Noël threw his arms akimbo, permitting himself total vulnerability, where the lion, not the trainer, was master.

Before the audience recovered, Noël went to an even larger feline and submerged himself in a chest-to-chest embrace that practically rendered the trainer invisible, so lost was he beneath the shaggy mane and chest fur of the animal. Nervous applause from the spectators was smothered quickly as Noël shoved his head into yet another lion's mouth in the same manner that he performed the first trick.

At that point the audience went wild. It was ready to expect anything from a trainer that was clearly teetering on the brink of insanity, so unpredictable were his actions. They weren't disappointed.

America has had its "wild" lion acts, as in the case of Clyde Beatty, and it has had acts of great beauty and gentleness, as in the case of Alfred Court and Charly Baumann, with their tigers. A few attempts have been made at capitalizing on the extroverted nature of lions to make a comic act, as in the case of Konyot, Zerbini, and a few others, but these have been weak attempts beside the efforts of the doughty Spaniard.

"What I do," Pablo said in a dressing-room interview, "is show le true nature of le lion. I show how gentle they can be. I show how they have fun, and I show ferocity. I put them all together and come out with le comedy."

"But what about injuries?" I asked. "Don't you run an unusually high risk by playing with your lions as if you are a lion yourself?"

"Si!" Pablo was on his feet, leaning to reveal a badly scarred shoulder. He rolled up his sleeve to show a pitted and gouged arm. "You know how many? Two hundred sixty-six! That's how many of the stitches!" He opened his eyes wide, as if in astonishment at the figure, and sat down again.

"Everything that I do is dangerous, with least danger in the tableaux. When les lions run back to les cages, they run over my body while I lie on the floor. And what about the sandwich?"

"Sandwich?"

"Si!" Pablo was on his feet again. "*Les deux* big lions lie down, and I run and jump on them so that we lie together, *ensemble* on the floor. Then a third comes off the stool and runs across the ring. She leaps on me, and we all roll around together. That's dangerous! But when I come out for applause I am smiling, and my lions are wiggling all over with happiness, because they have a good time, too. It is funny, but dangerous at the

same time. The audience knows that. The people like it."

"Have you ever had a really serious accident—I mean, one that incapacitated you?"

"Ah, *si*. But most of the accidents are little ones. Scratches. But once the big male, he clamped down when I stuck my head in his mouth."

"And?"

"Concussion. Fracture of le skull, and I lose my vision for seven hours." Noël waved his hand toward the floor, as if to dismiss the incident, and sat down again.

"I noticed that you bat your lions around a great deal. Because I know a little bit about lions myself, I can see that you couldn't possibly hurt them by this treatment. But what about animal protective organizations? Have you ever had any difficulties with them? Has anyone ever complained about your treatment of the cats?"

Noël's face glowered. He seemed to be stifling the impulse to explode. After allowing a reasonable length of time for his temper to subside he spoke again.

"No trouble in this country. In England they don't like whips, but that is because they do not understand. They do not see. I strike, yes—but not le lion. I strike *beside* le lion. What do you want, anyway? If I hit le lion he may kill me! Without Pablo, where is the act? It is foolish to claim I am cruel! How stupid!"

Noël was gathering steam again, and he spat out phrases in half French, half Spanish. He jumped from his seat and pretended to train lions in the dressing room. "Many people have no idea what *Les fauves* are like. Why do they make judgments? They think le lion, or le tigre is like—is like—a DOG!" He picked up a chair and slammed it on the floor for emphasis.

"The animal protective agencies—they go too far! They mix up *la force avec la brutalité*. They give the impression that they prefer animals over people."

"No. I no strike le lion. I strike *beside* him."

"Of course," I offered, in order to assure the Spaniard that I was not one of those who thought that way. "It is perfectly obvious . . ."

"*Brutalité?* Ha! You want brutalité you see lion acts in Spain, in Portugal, or in Italy! They like the blood and thunder; but not here, not in England, in France, in Germany. They know the animals in those countries. They go to see training."

"People are ignorant if they think le lion ou le tigre is like le dog. I have seen. In operations I have seen the skin of the big cat laid back. It is tough. It is thick, and is hard for the doctor to cut it, it is so tough. You have to work hard to hurt an animal like that."

"Mon ami," Pablo said, his eyes lowered and his voice a steely calm, "I know my job as you know yours. Why do people who are ignorant complain over something that they know nothing about?"

It was a question that I couldn't answer.

The names of some of Noël's lions are Bayar, Tarzan, Mouzi, Sultan, Nadia, Roma, and Napoli—the latter unaccountably named, for it was bought in Palermo, Italy. Three lions tower above the remaining seven in height, and are far bulkier. One was, I ventured, the largest female that I had ever seen. Her head was larger than Noël's entire chest.

"But you are wrong, *mon ami!* Le lion that you talk about is a male. Two lions without manes are males, and a third, also one of the largest, has a fine, shaggy mane!"

I stood corrected.

"You know of the remarkable trainer, Gunther Gebel-Williams?"

"Do I know him? I worked years with him in Germany."

"What is your opinion of him—of his training, I mean?"

"Gunther Williams is *un dompteur formidable.* But he is also an actor. He climbs onto the back of his *tigre,* on top of the elephant, and says to everybody—*C'est moi!*—It is me up here. See how remarkable I am! He is correct. He is remarkable—but he is also a remarkable actor.

"Me, I am a simpler artiste (*un artiste plus simple*). I like to give the public what pleases it most. They want to see lions and I give them lions. That is why I feel that the Scandinavian circuses, which do not allow wild animal acts, are not really circuses. Three things are asked for in a circus— *les fauves,* clowns, and trapeze acts. Without the wild beasts, it is not a circus.

"I am lucky to be here, with Ringling. It costs very much money to bring such an act as mine across the Atlantic to perform in America. I am very happy with Mr. Feld (the Ringling producer) and Mr. Feld is very happy with me. That is because I give the public what it wants. Besides, a great deal of money is spent just to take care of the cats. Can you imagine? All of those *tigres* in Charly Baumann's act, and ten big lions in my act as well? From ten to twenty pounds of meat a day are necessary to feed each of those animals,

and meat is expensive. Then there are the lions of Holzmair and the *tigres* of Williams on the other Ringling show. Now, a third is proposed. That's a lot of money! In Europe, we cannot believe all that money. But here in America it is so. It must be so. Here are the lions and *tigres* to prove it; and you see how beautiful they are! Not many animals in the circus are as beautiful as they are. It is an honor to appear with Ringling. Everybody in Europe wants to perform in America, but they cannot afford it.

"I have trained many animals. Leopards, and even hyenas. But there is only one animal for me, and that is le lion. My entire character is built for lions. I am one man outside the cage, and another when I enter with *les fauves.* If my wife will forgive me, there is one time when I am not married to her, and that is when I enter the cage with my lions. I am married to them, at that point. I think like they do, and work and play like they do. It is fun and it is beautiful. It is also dangerous; but it is as exciting to me as it is to the people who watch the act. They say, 'Pablo is crazy to do those things with the big cats.'—But no. Pablo is showing them what a lion is. He shows them that lions are not always serious, and that they love the performance just like the human artistes. Pablo shows them that people are only part of Nature. The wild beast is Nature, too; and we are all one. The thing to do is to enjoy this wonderful spectacle. People like that, and Pablo knows it."

Pablo does not compete with any other trainer. He enters into his own experience, and invites the public into it. He believes trainers are all the same, really—all workers. They may be more or less magnificent, but they are all workers at heart. According to Noël, that is good, because everybody is a worker finally, and workers, like trainers of *les fauves,* show audiences that they are not so far away from animals; and that animals are wonderful. They are part of Nature. Everything and everyone is part of Nature.

Exhausted by the interplay of half French, half Spanish, with limping English thrown in for good measure, I left my interview with Pablo Noël, my mind a whirl of miscellaneous facts and figures, but with the essence of the remarkable man's force very much influencing my thoughts and feelings. There could be little doubt that I had talked at length with one of the most brilliant practitioners of his craft. It was a vital and exciting experience —second only, perhaps, to the sight of the man they call Crazy Pablo mixing it up with his lions in the ring.

11

PERFORMING CHIMPANZEES

MY OPINION OF chimpanzees changed greatly once I had worked with them. Prior to my zoo experiences with the apes, I was a victim of their "ineffable charm" and devilish tomfoolery watching them in zoos or circuses. It was not until I had become involved in their care that I realized the volatile and dangerous nature of the beasts, their extremely complex psychological makeup, and their hair-trigger hysteria. The largest that I saw approached the size of fair-sized gorillas and were often truculent in nature. Their strength was impressive, as was their dental hardware, and I learned that the less I had to do with them the better.

Even before my feelings altered I wondered at chimps' popularity in the circus ring. I can remember watching a group of five presented by a portly man and wife who continually had difficulty keeping their charges under control, and ruined the act by disciplining the animals severely in front of the public. The chimps performed each routine with zest and ease, ran to the ring curb and extended their arms in the troupers' plea for applause. But following that they lost all interest, and simply sat there, vacantly gazing at the guy wires around them, not really a part of the act at all. They seemed bored.

Some time later I read a review of a circus performance that called chimpanzee trainers dropouts from a hairdresser's school—an unkind label, to be sure. But the statement made me realize that the trouble with the act I had seen earlier was not, in fact, the chimpanzee's fault. It was the trainer's failing, for the team that I remembered

did indeed seem like dropouts from *something*.

So it was that the opportunity to talk with chimp trainers who didn't seem like dropouts from anything at all came to me with genuine pleasure. The first trainers I spoke with were Sue and Rudy Lenz.

Seven chimps seemed to me like an inordinate number of animals to control, and I asked Sue if she could remember their names quickly, off the top of her head. Without hesitation she rattled off the names of Sally, Pancho, Andy, Pepe, Chico, Adair, and Joey. Sally, I was informed, was nine years old, and the elder of the troupe. When I expressed surprise at a nine-year-old chimp being trustworthy enough to perform in the ring, Sue frowned at me, disbelieving.

"No," she said, "it all depends on the individual. I mean, you can get one that's vicious at six, or maybe another that's a love at twelve. It's strictly individual. Chimps, you know, are really people in monkey costumes. Some are aggressive and some are not, but once in a while you get a stinker. There are more stinkers in the human race than there are in chimps, I'd say."

She knew whereof she spoke, for the Lenz chimp act has been performing for eighteen years, and was a staple with England's great Bertram Mills Circus until it closed.

I was curious about practical problems encountered in the ring, and asked particularly about a routine in which a chimp stands on its hands atop two poles, that are held by a motorized boat driven around the ring.

"Well, you know, we do have problems with

that. The aerialist that follows us has equipment hanging over the ring, and one time I drove the boat in too big a circle. A rope knocked the little chimp off his handstand. It didn't hurt him, or anything like that, but ever since that day the chimp looks around as he stands on his hands. He wants to know where that dratted rope is—just to get back at it, to get even. Whenever he gets near the rope he tries to grab it. That rocks the boat and causes problems. He doesn't do the routine perfectly unless the rigging is higher than it is here."

Sue then drifted off into a description of the chimps' diet. Claiming first that everybody feeds their chimps differently, she listed the exotic menu offered the Lenz troupe. Feeling that chimps are "like us" and therefore crave variety, she starts the day off by giving her charges apples. At twelve o'clock they are given bananas, and at four o'clock oranges and grapefruit are offered. Next comes a meal that is always different. One day it may be grapes, or another it may be a complete mixed salad, including cucumbers, lettuce, grapes, chickory, or corn on the cob. The important thing is that the animals never know what the meal will be. At night the chimps have a pint and a half of tea each, along with half a loaf of bread.

"What kind of tea?"

"English. Ty-Phoo tea. My mother sends eighteen pounds of it over to us when we need it, because it's hard to locate here. With the chimps we did six television commercials for tea in England, but it was very embarrassing, because it wasn't Ty-Phoo tea! After the commercials, I had to buy the tea we advertised and stick it in the cupboards of the trailer so that people would see that we used their tea!"

Within their own unit, the Lenz's have no discipline problems. But trouble in other rings invariably spills over and gives the Lenz troupe problems as well. The close, family unity of the Lenz troupe makes genuine discipline problems rare.

In order to promote this unity, Rudy and Sue Lenz purchase a new, young chimp and keep it for six months with no training whatsoever. They feel that they can afford to do this because they have a full complement of performing chimps in any case. When bought, a new chimp is usually either very vicious or very scared. During the six-month waiting period the new arrival can get to know its owners and they can understand the animal as well. The chimp is given time to build its confidence. If a specimen shows that he continually fears people, he is traded before the end of the adjustment period. But if he looks like he might work out, he is taught two simple tricks. Applause is one, and performing on an instrument in the chimp bandstand is the other. The animal is then taken into the ring, to see how the public reacts to it, and how it reacts to the public.

"It's pointless spending all the time training a chimp difficult or complicated tricks and then taking it into the ring to find that it will always be terrified of the audience. It could amount to a big waste of time if the chimp freezes in front of the audience. We always think psychologically first, and train later.

"Some of our tricks are really hard, you know, and couldn't be taught a newcomer quickly anyway. Like the iron jaw, where the chimp hangs by his teeth and swivels around in the air. We thought to ourselves how it would be if we were learning it. We knew we would get sore in our neck muscles. We can say when we hurt, but an animal can't; so we took six months to train our chimp to do that one trick. We wanted to build up his muscles so gradually that no question of pain would enter into the situation at all. Otherwise the chimp wouldn't like to do the trick, and a chimp must first of all *want* to perform."

All of the Lenz chimps tend to be young because of the difficulty in handling chimps once they arrive at maturity.

"Why do chimps become difficult when they reach a certain age, some of them?" Sue asked rhetorically. "Because they are grown-ups, and don't want to be told what to do any more. They want to breed. That's not so unusual, after all. We've heard of chimps performing in their twenties, but we think that's ridiculous. When a grown-up bites you, you're gonna lose fingers! So what's the sense in keeping 'em? The thing to do is to let them breed. We pension ours off to zoos that meet our specifications, and have a lot placed in England. Our last pensioner is in Switzerland. I mean, we've had work out of him. Why not let him live the remainder of his life normally? Isn't that better than beating the daylights out of a chimp that doesn't want to perform?

"Take our big chimp, Sally. We'll keep her as long as she's good. We've got a beautiful thing going, Sally and me. We both idolize each other, and no young chimp will ever take the place of that. In a discussion once, somebody said that they didn't think chimps could think, and I could have hit him then and there. As an example of their thinking there is a case with Sally. We dress the chimps first, then change our costumes right in the chimp wagon. Sally holds my costume for me, then hands it to me when I am ready to put it on. She does the same thing in reverse, when I get back into street clothes.

"But two years ago a new chimp act came into the end ring with enormous chimps, and Sally looked over from her seat in the center ring. She kept shouting at them, sort of trying to decide who was the toughest chimp, herself or the newcomers. I threatened her to keep her quiet. I didn't smack her, because she was only doing what comes naturally. But I became very angry at her, and didn't speak to her for a number of days except to order her around in a rough voice when I had to. It broke my heart more than it did hers, I'm sure. Well one day I was getting dressed and I handed her my costume to hold, but I didn't talk with her. She looked at me for a minute and threw it on the floor! You can't tell me that Sally didn't think. She was saying, in her head, that if I wasn't going to talk to her, then to hell with the bloody costume!

"As long as she behaves, and as long as she and I have this mutual admiration society going for us, we'll keep her. But after that she'll be treated to the married life of a normal chimp, and she deserves it."

Generally in agreement with Sue and Rudy Lenz was Mickey Antalek, another chimp trainer with Ringling Bros. Circus. His act uses three, somewhat larger chimps, and is notable for its wildness and freedom. Chimps scurry to the top of a pole balanced on Mickey's head, to perform handstands while applauding with their feet. They are pulled high in the air on Roman rings, much like human aerialists (and far outdo their human counterparts with their gyrations.) They perform a killingly funny parody of a bullfight, with one chimp wearing appliquéd horns, and finally scoring a bull's eye on Mickey's behind, as he stoops to adjust the cape of the fighter. The act is fast paced and unusually successful with its humor.

Although some chimp trainers operate too "tightly" with their charges, according to Mickey, he is able to obtain better results by allowing his chimps room for their freewheeling, zany antics. This is partly to make them happy, because he believes that no chimp performing because he is scared will ever last very long in the ring and remain trustworthy.

"Chimps are great at communicating with people without words," Mickey said. "The audience would know at once if a chimp was being treated badly, or didn't enjoy what he was doing. When an audience realizes that, the feeling of disapproval towards the trainer can be felt throughout the entire auditorium. An act like that doesn't usually last."

Mickey feeds his chimps differently from the Lenz troupe, and explained that just about every trainer feeds differently from every other. The Antalek chimps start out with cooked oatmeal, flavored with either honey or sugar. They next receive bread and jam, or sweet rolls. On work days, after the matinee, they have orange juice or orange drinks. Before the night performance, Mickey makes all of the fruit buckets ready. These are offered after the night show, and include a wide variety of both fruits and vegetables. The chimps get vitamins only if they are "down" and need building up.

Mickey once had to get rid of a chimp due to its jealousy.

"He was OK with me, but was jealous of the other chimps," he said. "Like we had this big motorcycle, and he loved it, but he wouldn't let any of the other chimps on it."

Antalek's approach to the introduction of a new chimp into the act parallels, in its way, that of the Lenzes. The most important thing is to allow the chimp to have faith in its trainer, to enjoy association with him, and to trust him. This is a continual process, beginning with the newcomer's arrival and continuing through to his older chimps. The bond is continually fostered by little verbal reminders of affection, pats, and expressions of trust from the trainer for the entire duration of the chimp's stay with the act.

Mickey claims that his chimps are always laughing at something or other while they are performing. He can't find out what it is, but he is satisfied that they are having fun while in the ring, which is an important factor in successful training. He began with chimps two years before he signed with Ringling, and developed the act in Shrine circuses. He has been with Ringling ever since. Rather than attempt to introduce a totally new routine during the circus's brief rest period, he introduces new variations little by little during the season. This, he feels, is a big step forward in the long run, although just a slight improvement on a daily basis. He trains gradually as he performs.

"Chimps have definite preferences about many

Doubling in brass as horse trainer, Evy Althoff poses Ringling's Blue Unit horses along the ring curb.

Tiger and trainer drop simultaneously from a standing position, forming a final pose.

Hail, Conquering Hero Holzmair!

things," Mickey said. "They all love the big, new motorcycle, and they all adored it from the beginning. That's because it is big and shiny like the last one, but it has more room. But when we first started we had one chimp and a bicycle. It was a blue bike, and that cussed chimp wouldn't have anything to do with it. He screamed, and threw it out of the ring. We had an awful time. Well, human beings are often slower than animals in understanding things, you know, and I finally got to thinking that maybe it was the color that upset him. So I painted it red. The day after it dried he sat on it and gave no further trouble. The thing was, he just didn't like blue!"

Although no difficulties have arisen with his chimps biting or misbehaving, Antalek is interrupted, once in a while, by disruptions in other rings. Sometimes, when such a thing happens, one of his chimps will scream in fear. But Mickey doesn't have to do anything about it because another chimp always goes to the upset one and puts his arms around him in order to calm him down.

In 1970, chimps were in the two end rings and a large bear act was in the center. One of the bears escaped and dashed across the ring full of chimps on its way out the door. Mickey and his chimps, at the opposite end of the arena, remained unaware of the incident, for the Antalek chimps are kept busy every minute they are in the ring, and are totally absorbed in what they are doing. A happy trio, they seem satisfied that they have their own thing going for them right where they are.

I came from my interview with these two masterful chimp trainers with a feeling far different from that when I had talked with trainers of the big cats. I felt that I had not talked with a trainer and his pupils at all, but that I had spent a few minutes with two perfectly happy performing families. Although both the Lenzes and the Antaleks would undoubtedly disclaim the idea that there is a single key that unlocks the secret of training chimpanzees, my impression is that consideration of the animals as fellow performers and as individuals with their own rights and preferences goes a long way toward the making of a successful chimp act. Maybe, after all, the chimp-human combination is what is meant when the circus is referred to as "family entertainment"!

12

THE REPUBLICANS

THERE ARE SO many aspects about the behavior of elephants and so many variations within species, that sensible discussion about them is difficult on a popular level. They are divided into two species. One of these is the Asiatic or Indian elephant, that carries the scientific label of *Elephas maximus*. I like that name enormously, for it seems full of implications. It seems to advertise what an elephant should be.

The beast itself does not disappoint us. Its head and body length can measure over 19 feet, and its shoulder height can be from 7 to 10 feet. Although the head is higher, it is bobbed up and down with such frequency that it cannot be used as a proper, scientific height measurement. Weight, as listed in reliable journals, is "about 5½ tons."

Externally, the Indian elephant can be identified at once by its relatively small ears, high, domelike forehead and sloping hindquarters. There are usually four toenails on the hind feet. The highest point of the back is between the shoulder and pelvis. This placement gives the animal a slightly humped appearance.

The African elephant is known by the scientific name of *Loxodonta africana*. It has been recorded as "up to 13 feet," considerably taller than its Asiatic cousin. Its weight is from almost 5½ to over 8 tons. The taller height of the African elephant is due, sensibly enough, to its longer legs. The entire animal presents a thinner appearance than does the Indian elephant. Its forehead is markedly less convex and it possesses no bulging brows. The high points of the African elephant's

back are located at its shoulders and pelvis, and the animal seems to sag between these girdles. If one could get close enough, he could see that the African elephant has but three toenails on its hind feet.

The single, most distinctive characteristic of *Loxodonta* is its enormous, fanlike ears. It can carry these flat alongside its shoulders or, when alarmed, at right angles to its body in order to increase the efficiency of its directional hearing. These ears have been measured at five feet from top to bottom.

A subtler difference between Indian and African elephants can be found in the tips of their respective trunks. The African elephant has a fingerlike projection both above and below its trunk tip; the Indian elephant has but one such projection. These structural differences do not seem to increase or decrease either animal's efficiency when it grasps for peanuts from a zoo visitor.

The label of "hose-nose," sometimes given to elephants by jokers, is tellingly correct, for the animals drink by filling their trunks with water before squirting it into their mouths, and also give themselves shower baths in the same manner. African elephants seeking relief from the heat of the veldt direct their trunk-hoses first towards their massive ears, which are filled with tiny veins. Blood cooled by the spray then circulates through the animal's body. There is little doubt that the elephant's trunk is the most remarkable mammalian appendage known, far exceeding the prehensile tails of some animals in its wonder and complexity.

The odor of both species of elephant seems to be both identical and overwhelming, for they have an ammonialike scent revolting to many humans. But this is the same odor that causes a ripple of excitement among children just before an elephant act is announced at the circus, so I suppose that there can be no accurate accounting for its presentability.

The wild elephant, whether African or Indian, is majestic in aspect, deliberate, and massively beautiful in its actions, and probably doomed as another victim of the encroachment of "civilization." It is not due to its size that we sense the enormity of the vacuum created by the eventual extinction of such a significant and gentle beast. Films of elephant behavior in the wild have shown us what only a few could have seen prior to the invention of television, and we have been moved and awed by the insights given us. We wonder how any hunter, for any reason, could center his rifle's sights on those vast, grey-brown hulks. But we have wondered from afar. Our sympathies and opinions have been secondhand. What about those elephants closer to us—in captivity?

Visiting two of the smaller zoos of New York City, I found that they exhibited elephants that are not elephants at all, as far as I am concerned. The beasts exist in sterile cells, with little more than outdoor, prisoner's walkarounds for exercise. In some cases the animals were adored by the public at the same time they were loathed by their keepers. They were undisciplined and sometimes browbeaten in or out of their stalls if bribery failed. At first I felt that the keepers were at fault, and perhaps, sometimes, they were. But on closer investigation I learned that zoo elephants are usually excess baggage from the circus world. They may be sold to zoos because they are cantankerous or unreliable. No circus could expose such animals to the public at semiliberty with a clear conscience for very long; so the animals are placed "in retirement" in various zoos around the country. This guarantees that nearly all of America's elephant population is female, for females (called bulls in circuses) are considered to be the safest elephants for use in performances. Female elephants do not suffer from violent temper tantrums, as do males when they go through a period called musth. At this time glands in the elephant's temples exude an oily liquid that runs down the animal's cheeks, finally dribbling into the beast's mouth. "Elephant men" have suggested that the vitriolic taste of this fluid drives the animal into a temporary state of madness, making it mortally dangerous for anyone attempting to work with elephants in this condition.

Portland, Oregon, possesses a famous male elephant that has successfully sired many babies. The Portland bull is in great demand as a stud animal—so much so that the zoo's facilities have been severely strained by boarding visiting female pachyderms and by the elephant babies in Portland's own herd. Visitors, too, have clogged the facilities of the Portland Zoo. "Packy" 's fame has spread so far that an entirely new parking lot has been constructed to accommodate his fans.

Among animal handlers, elephants are considered to be special beasts, and so need special keepers. Slow to form attachments, elephants are even slower to give them up once they are in effect. A sudden change of keeper can spell disaster, for there is a great deal of devotion in an animal as big as an elephant and a great deal of violence when it feels robbed of the object of its affection.

Some years ago the tiny zoo in Scranton, Pennsylvania, housed an elephant and a donkey together in the same stall. The elephant could scarcely be handled and kept the donkey in the rear of its stall, far from intrusion by the keepers. The donkey could not be reached. Gradually its unmanicured hooves recurved so badly that they nearly pierced its legs. No one could get near the donkey to correct the situation because it was jealously defended by the elephant. Signs on the cage warned visitors to stand back because the elephant was dangerous. It could and did lash out with its trunk and throw objects at zoo visitors. The whole, sorry mess was the result of lack of discipline. The elephant had simply not found the right keeper, one who was firm but showed genuine affection for the animal as well. I understand that the animal finally had to be shot.

Frankly, I am leery of elephants—with good reason.

Once, when I made an abortive attempt at a circus career in my younger days, I was assigned the task of holding the folded train attached to a huge elephant blanket worn by an enormous, benevolently inclined elephant named Jewel in the Ringling circus herd. Directly behind Jewel came the final elephant in the procession, named Marcella. She wore gigantic, wooden wings over her blanket, that were affixed to her body by means of a steel harness. The wings weighed perhaps two hundred pounds each.

A fellow worker and myself were told to carry

the folded train up the ramp of the old 50th Street Madison Square Garden. (The menagerie was located in the basement of that magnificent building, and the performing arena was one flight up.) When we reached the arena entrance, costumed attendants were to take the train from us, unfold it, and march around the hippodrome.

Our position in the tunnel-like ramp was a crowded one, and we were forced to stand beside Marcella while we held Jewel's train. We were located on Marcella's right side, a position that most elephants dislike because they are trained to accept handlers on the left. Marcella, uneasy under these crowded conditions, started to sway back and forth, an action that brought the heavy wings within a foot of our faces—much too close for comfort. As the swaying continued, visions of being crushed against the wall passed through my mind, and I thought it best to make my presence known to the bull. Summoning as much volume as I could, I shouted "Ho!" and kicked Marcella soundly on her right front foot. She scarcely budged, but her handler peered around from the left side and told me to take it easy. He hinted broadly that I might make Marcella nervous with possible dire consequences.

As the swaying was resumed, I was not assured. Neither was my cohort, who hastily dumped the entire train into my arms and fled. Scarcely able to support the weight of the train, I watched as the wooden wings came closer and closer to me. Finally, Marcella swayed away from me and held her body poised for a moment. I sensed that a heavy shove would follow that action, and that the elephant was gathering her efforts to squash the annoying greenhorn on her right. I dropped silently onto the ramp floor just behind her right front foot.

Marcella crashed against the wall with a reverberating noise that sent spangles flying all over the floor. The handler (a good one, fortunately) gave the bull a tug with his hook and made her back up a few paces. I got up, gathered Jewel's train, and followed the parade up the ramp. Marcella knew that she had a perfect foil in front of her and whacked wickedly against my heels at each step all the way to the hippodrome door!

Years later at the zoo in Boston, Massachusetts, I related this incident to its talented elephant man, Tom Veasey. He roared with laughter.

"Hell, Herb," he said, "Marcella was nervous, that's all. I broke that elephant myself, years ago, and she never was a tail elephant."

I asked him what he meant by the term.

"Why, she was a lead bull from the word go. She hadda be out in front and was always upset when there was nothing behind her. That, plus the fact that she was all crowded up in that damned tunnel and had a nervous little geek like yourself to the right of her, was all just too much for her."

I believed him, but swore that I would never go near that elephant again.

Fourteen years after my conversation with Veasey, while talking with the Ringling elephant trainer Hugo Schmitt, I idly handed peanuts to several elephants nearby.

"Giff her anudder vun, dat vun dere," the stocky German instructed me. "She's a gut girl!, vun uff da lest uff da olt vuns. Chewel, she up unt died, but dat vun dere, she's Marcella. I bring her alonk becuss she likes it, unt vud miss da life on da road, but I only youse her in da parade. Nichts in da act."

I did as I was told, but felt a little uneasy as I handed her the peanut.

I am sure that my uneasiness was noted by the great and ancient beast, although she didn't show it. Hugo was there, and his barrel-chested presence was more than enough to intimidate the elephant. Any thoughts of wrongdoing quit the elephantine mind immediately if the boss is around.

Schmitt has been called a martinet with his elephant pupils by more than one circus performer, but obvious, sometimes even sentimental, concern for his charges was still there in 1971 when things were going to suit him. During that year, after which Schmitt retired from the ring, the circus was less gargantuan than in former years, and the trainer governed a herd of seventeen or eighteen elephants. Perhaps this smaller number mellowed Hugo, for the old days saw him under the enormous pressure of handling a herd of fifty-five bulls. Each had its handler, of course, but the unified and total control, as well as the final word, was Schmitt's.

Most head trainers, like Schmitt, use many subordinate handlers for control of the herd. A brilliant exception to this custom occurred in 1969, when the Ringling Circus brought Gunther Gebel-Williams to America. He came with his own group of animal acts, around which a new Ringling unit (the Red Unit) was formed.

Williams used the entire arena for his elephant act after first performing several remarkable routines with a few bulls in the center ring. The

Ringling

Baggage wagon, menagerie cages, and hippo den of Ringling Bros. Circus show how heavy rolling stock was in the 1950s—prior to the circus's move indoors. (Author's photos)

audience noticed immediately that there were not many individual handlers in the arena. There were perhaps two or three jogging beside the seventeen massive bulls, as they hurried around the hippodrome. Suddenly the band fell silent as Gunther's voice bellowed from the center ring. Each elephant stopped in its tracks as if struck by a locomotive, settled back onto a tub and reared to an upright, sitting position—*on the vocal commands of one trainer!* Nobody jerked the elephants into position with a bull hook, or "whapped" a nearby beast to "remind" it of its duties. The sole motivating force stood in the center ring, very much in control. The audience went crazy with applause, and America had found a new circus star.

The heights of training reached by Gebel-Williams are dealt with elsewhere. At this point it is enough to mention the presence of an African elephant in his act. In the fifties, Schmitt had used an African elephant, advertised as a pigmy, but it was withdrawn after a few years. Williams's elephant is young, lively, and, as might be expected, beautifully controlled. Spectators were thunderstruck at a performance in New Haven, Connecticut, when the animal walked from the end of the arena to the center ring, mounted a tub and

A Ringling calliope, refurbished for a tour in the 1950s. (Author's photo)

revolved around on it, entirely without a trainer. Williams stood in the wings, watching. The only visible control was his presence. Yet his animals exhibit nothing but fondness for him, and undertake their performances with a sense of camaraderie and verve that indicates a togetherness with their trainer that is based upon affection.

While accustomed to performing elephants, most Americans are unaware of the animals' employment as stevedores. The elephant's role as a work animal in America is almost exclusively with the circus, except for the famous publicity stunt undertaken by Barnum, when he had a work elephant plow his farmlands alongside the New Haven Railroad tracks that ran from Boston to New York. This was merely off-season employment for the bull, which was otherwise engaged in customary laborer's work on the circus lot. Many a show would not have arrived at its next town had it not been for the yeoman's efforts of its pachyderms, pulling and pushing wagons from muck that often reached higher than the hubcaps of the wagons. Elephants are well equipped for sloshing in thick mud, because their feet have spongy soles. When they plant their impressive weight upon their feet, the feet expand. When the weight is released, the feet contract. This prevents elephants from becoming stuck in any but the most extreme circumstances.

Ringling's historic Bell Wagon is now on display at the Ringling Circus Museum in Sarasota, Florida. (Author's photo)

The famous Long Mount, as performed by Hugo Schmitt's "bulls" in the 100th Anniversary of Ringling Bros. Circus.

The arrival of the automobile displaced most elephants as laborers on the circus lot, a displacement carried further by the demise of the larger circuses as outdoor, tented operations. But today this role may still be seen in abbreviated form, if one visits the lots of any of the country's smaller towns.

In 1970, I watched as Shandra, lead bull of the Circus Bartok herd, waited patiently inside the big top, while all but the two center poles and the sidewall poles were removed by hand. She was then hitched by a long chain (fastened onto her heavy shoulder harness) to the base of one of the two aluminum center poles. Given the command to run, she did so with a reverberating bellow. The base of the pole was yanked in her direction, and the pole fell to the ground away from her. She stopped beneath the second pole, and was hitched to its base. A second command to run brought Shandra out from under the edge of the canvas with another roar, as the pole fell

away to the ground and the tent billowed down.

Shandra was also used to remove the stakes from the ground around the perimeter of the tent. This was done by use of a harness around her shoulders that was fastened to a length of chain that hung beneath her head. The chain was flipped twice around each stake as the elephant stood patiently by. Shandra, who probably knew her job better than her trainer, leaned forward and gave an upward and backward tug with her shoulders. The stake popped out of the ground as if the earth had been made of butter.

But every evidence indicates that the time that circus elephants love best, aside from sleeping and eating, is the time spent performing. The enormous psychological bonus that comes from audience reaction appears to be as effective on animals as it is on human performers. This, when added to the exercise afforded by performance, is one of the forces that keeps elephants trouping. After all, what are silly little stakes and insignificant chains on their legs to elephants? I have seen elephants in the Ringling herd snap chains from the concrete floor of the menagerie in New York City, when their sisters had gone into the ring. They didn't go anywhere. They merely wanted to know that they were not restrained by force when their cohorts had left the area.

"Doc" Bartok put it correctly when he pointed out an enormous bull in the herd that was standing, totally unrestrained, in the circus's backyard. "Been that way all day, and never leaves. She hangs around because she likes it, that's why. We must be doing something right!"

A clown in spec costume gazes at the audience before the show begins.

Madison Square Garden as it appeared set up for the 100th Anniversary production of Ringling Bros. Circus.

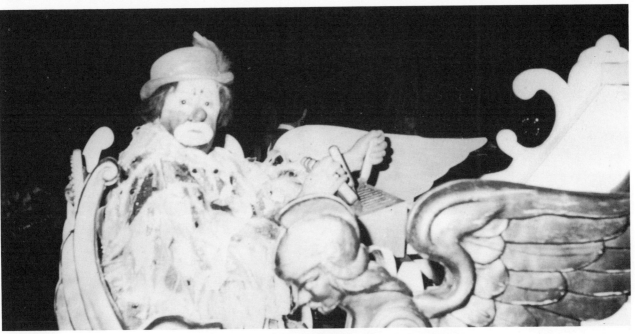

Otto Griebling, the finest pantomime clown yet to appear in any American circus, was given a tramp suit of silver tatters for his role in the 100th Anniversary spec.

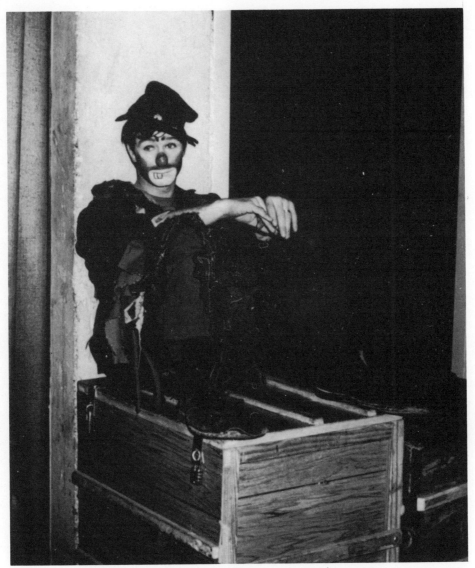

Exhaustion prompts a candid pose of wearisome tranquility by an anonymous Ringling clown.

Billy Stephenson chases a "runaway" dog around the ring curb. Such vitality and pep are trademarks of the Stephensons' dog act—billed simply as the greatest in the world.

Doubling in brass as horse trainer, Evy Althoff poses Ringling's Blue Unit horses along the ring curb.

In 1970, Ringling's Red Unit tried out a comedy routine performed by Pio Nock and Company.

One of Althoff's deft and shaggy pupils.

Flo Stephenson returns from the ring.

Ringling's 100th Anniversary spec was brilliantly conceived and produced.

Billy Baker virtually dances through his routine with Ringling's horses.

Clad in gypsy attire show girls, grooms, and Hugo Schmitt parade around the hippodrome track for the presentation of the elephant act.

Perched atop a recumbent and complaining fellow-performer, a Ringling elephant dwarfs trainer Schmitt.

Billy and Dinah Stephenson, here shown as the Riding Saxons, check performance details before entering the ring.

Flo Stephenson is as excited over her poodle's successful performance as the audience.

13

JOKERS

I HAVE READ a great deal about clowns and have seen them perform many times. Long ago I felt that they were oversold by romantic writers who remembered what "funny" was in the old days. It seemed to me that every clown was treated as a classic, worth retaining simply for the sake of the clowning art. I still feel this way, to a degree. But I have come to the point where I can sift an ordinary clown from the company of his fellow artists. Just as every violin player is not a Heifetz, and every club singer cannot be a Piaf, so every clown cannot be a Grock, a Popov, or a Griebling.

In my youth I carefully studied texts that dealt with clown types. Authors, when concerned with the subject of clowning, seemed to have the distressing habit of delving into what they claimed to be history; and I waded glumly through pages dealing with *Commedia del' Arte* buffoonery, classical, Grecian and Roman dwarfs, and traveling bands of Romanys.

I was utterly bored.

Without the least trace of irreverence to the memory of the great Dan Rice, I submit that what makes a clown a good one is his ability to make people smile and laugh. This was historically true of the great clowns of the past, and their stories are interesting from the point of view of curiosity. But just as their humor was unique to their own time, ours is unique to ours. Today they would not be great clowns, in my opinion, without a marked updating of their routines.

Clowns are divided basically into three types. One is the Joey, who may be white-faced or may

simply have exaggerated features on his face like a rubber ball nose. The feature that makes a Joey a Joey is his acrobatic skill. A Joey is the clown who actually performs, and is often featured in such routines as bareback riding acts. The second type of clown is called the Auguste. This is the typical, white-faced prankster featured so prominently in clown walkarounds. Augustes have little routines they perform periodically during their peregrinations. Some take part in clown production numbers that are genuinely clever and funny. Magic is often used, but small magic tricks are not often successful in the large arenas where American circuses perform. Only if they are performed with rhythm and flair, sometimes in conjunction with a clown sidekick, do they really succeed.

The third type of clown is the Charlie. He is the tramp clown, said to have been based upon Chaplin's character. These clowns often use pathos as their gambit. They are frequently real character studies, achieved through complex development of character traits during years of study. There are quite a few unsuccessful Charlies in the ring currently. Some dress like a Charlie, but perform like an Auguste—a sure path to second class in clowndom!

But these classic types have become so bastardized that they rarely appear in pure form, except as a novelty. When a clown ceases to *relate* he begins to belong to the past, and to take his place in that wonderfully garbled hodgepodge of circus history.

Some of the greatest American clowns didn't

spend the larger part of their careers in circuses at all. W. C. Fields, Charlie Chaplin, and Bert Lahr were all great clowns. Just as great clowns do not belong especially to the circus, good clowning is often found in other arenas than those filled with tanbark (or its latter-day replacement, the rubber mat). Indeed, ordinary people, going about their regular daily chores, sometimes create bits of clowning that can legitimately be regarded as inspired. A fun-filled person, spotting a battered umbrella in the gutter, may well manipulate it and "carry on" with it in a way that equals the ridiculous antics of a highly trained professional. Perhaps it would be better to say that this person equals a professional clown in every respect—except one; this practical joker of a citizen is usually doing exactly that—pulling a practical joke. Good clowning does not consist of pulling off jokes, although many routines are built around punch-line situations that are close to practical gags. Relying heavily on intuitive inspiration, good clowning is a personality study of the practical joker, rather than the actual performance of such a joke. Character studies make good clowning, but simply being a "character" does not.

One of my favorite clowns was Otto Griebling, the Ringling tramp who replaced the internationally famous tramp clown, Emmett Kelly. In my opinion, Griebling was always superior to Kelly because he *did* something. Kelly's forte was in being "done in" by the worldly forces around him, and sadly yielding to his fate; but Griebling, equally the loser, was outraged at his fate. He went down fighting mad, and related to thousands of us in the bargain. Griebling's preperformance work with the audience was a classic that has been imitated many times, but never equalled. He strode into the empty arena, his tattered jacket and pants so frayed and filthy that they could have stood by themselves—if there had been enough threads to support them. (It is said that Griebling cultivated, rather than cleaned his clothes.) Noisily banging tin pie plates together, he directed the audience's attention to him at once, apparently under the impression that *he* was what they came to see. He stepped close to the audience and juggled the plates briefly. The crowd applauded. He listened to the handclapping critically, shrugged as if he wasn't quite satisfied with it, and plodded across the ring to the audience on the other side. Extending his hands toward the spectators that he had just left, and swiping his arms earthward in an ultimate gesture of rejection, he repeated

his juggling routine. His new audience got the idea at once, and applauded with more verve than its predecessor. Delighted, Griebling scuttled happily back to his earlier audience and gestured to them, telling that the people across the way did better than they, themselves, did, and suggested to them that he was about to give them a second chance. Now in open competition with the spectators across the arena from them, the members of the audience prepared to demonstrate their appreciation as the clown juggled again. This time the ovation was thunderous, and Griebling was ecstatic. He offered the crowd his ultimate response by grasping the edge of his filthy jacket as Queen Elizabeth might arrange her train, and performed a curtsy so ridiculously delicate that audiences have become convulsed while seeing it.

Secure in his triumph, he gazed at the crowds across the ring again. Should he leave his present haven of wild applause and risk the reception from the other side? He took off his hat and scratched his head, looking first at one side of the house, then at the other. Finally he decided to take the plunge, and ventured across the ring. His routine was greeted by frenetic cheers, screams, and a deluge of applause that far outweighed his earlier reception. At this he pretended to pick up a pie plate full of sawdust and throw it nastily towards the side of the audience that offered the lesser applause. (In the old days, when sawdust chips were used, he actually did throw a plateful.)

Griebling often performed this routine at the end of the arena, where he could work three sides of the house against each other. He purposely ignored the fact that he himself soon became lost in the competition as each segment of the audience tried to outdo its opponent. Under such conditions, his frenzied zeal and pomposity became doubly hilarious.

In earlier routines, Griebling was forever seeking a lady by the name of Mrs. Schultz. One such search involved the delivery of a thirty-pound cake of ice. Since he never found her, his ice tongs were holding nothing but an ice cube by the time he gave up his search, after periodic appearances, late in the performance. A similar search for Mrs. Schultz involved a potted plant that he was to deliver to her. By the end of the performance the plant was so huge that it was wheeled around in a wheelbarrow by a visibly aged and exhausted Griebling. He never did deliver it, of course.

Another delivery routine was part of Griebling's repertoire in the 1970s. In it he ambled around carrying what must surely have been the most decayed, crumbled, and decomposed parcel-post package ever to have existed. He also carried a tattered pad and pencil. The route took him along the hippodrome, in front of the boxes. Finally he stopped before a (preferably wealthy) patron, studied her minutely and searched through his pad. Finding her name, he then made a vicious slash across the pad—as if she was not worthy of the delivery—and ambled on to another location. This slash, as simple as it was, certainly was the most positive, angry, and belligerent expression of rejection that I have ever seen. Lines of outrage creased his face as he performed the act. I have seen patrons visibly upset by it before they caught themselves, remembering that the whole affair was patently false—mere clowning.

I sat ringside with a young lady who was eating some ice cream during a performance of the circus in Boston. Along came Griebling, who paused, leaned on the railing and commenced dusting it with a rag that was filthier than papers on a pet shop floor. Slowly, as he gazed at my companion, his dusting stopped until he appeared to be lost in adulation. He simply stared at her. Her reactions were too violent and embarrassed to control. She laughed helplessly, of course, but she couldn't face the tramp's steady gaze. She dropped ice cream onto the floor, missed her mouth as she tried to take another bite, and finally thrust a spoonful at the clown, averting her face and closing her eyes as she did so. She was so embarrassed that she was a perfect foil for the master clown.

Griebling delighted in popping up, here and there during the performance, lampooning acts that were going on in the rings, or offering editorial comment on them. He didn't often approve. I can remember when he was dressed in a gunny-sack robe, Hindu style, wearing a turban that was too large for him. He "clowned" the entire, opulent procession that paraded around him. As costly floats, trappings, and costumes marched sedately by, he bowed and scraped to the audience, thumping his chest to emphasize that *he* was the real attraction of the parade—and indeed he was. When the final assemblage of gorgeously robed elephants passed by, he held his nose; as the cast stood along the hippodrome, their arms extended outwards and upwards in the traditional circus appeal for applause, Griebling lowered himself to the tanbark in a Hindu gesture of supplication, touching the sawdust with his nose. Amid all of

the glitter and largesse, every eye was on Griebling, who seemed to be nothing more than a shapeless pile of burlap, lost amid the grandeur but sticking out like a sore thumb (by virtue of his tattered rags) at the same time. It was the only Ringling spec that I can remember which ended by the audience laughing as it applauded.

If, as one clown maintains, clowning becomes an insatiable search for the perfect detail, the right gesture, the quintessential bit of business, then there can be no question about who stood atop the heap of fools in 1970. It was Otto Griebling, whose seventy-fourth birthday was celebrated when the circus played its one-hundredth anniversary stand in Madison Square Garden. The New York showing had many highlights, but chief among them was a matinee performance on the twenty-eighth of April. Before the performance began, Otto performed his audience warm-up to an enthusiastic house. As the performance got ready to begin he was whistled off as usual. But the performance did not start. Instead, the mellifluous voice of the circus announcer, Harold Ronk, told the spectators that it was Otto Griebling's birthday. The announcement so took Griebling by surprise that he left the arena with tears in his eyes. But it was more than just an announcement. It was truly an acknowledgment on the part of the entire circus company, gathered from all over the world, that Griebling, one among a company considered to be the cream of the crop, was the best that there was. It was, to Otto, a testimony of admiration from his peers.

That the most magnificent circus anywhere, in the richest country in the world, could single out a man like Griebling for its applause is remarkable enough. But what must it have felt like to a man who started out the son of a grocer in Coblenz, who was left fatherless at thirteen, and whose mother migrated to America, leaving him a poverty-stricken apprentice to a demanding and ungenerous bareback rider?

As was the custom with the European apprentice system, the title owner got the money, leaving the apprentice with board, room, instruction—and work.

After some time under this apprenticeship, word was received from Griebling's mother that she had become established in America, and could support Otto if he could get to her. He left his employer at a German port, signing on as a mess boy on a trans-Atlantic freighter that he thought was headed to New York, but which went, instead, to Japan! Nine months later he straggled into New York City, worked briefly at another job, then signed as an apprentice to Hodgini, an English equestrian then appearing with Ringling. This apprenticeship was no better than the first, and left Otto still unhappy, still undecided, and still yearning for full-fledged circus life on his own. He worked as a rider for Tom Mix, Sells Floto, and, in 1929, toured outdoor fairs performing clown riding together with gymnastics. But in 1930, he fell, breaking his legs in two places, along with his wrist. Riding, from that point on, was out. His career as a Joey was finished.

It was in the hospital, while convalescing, that Otto decided to devote all of his efforts towards clowning. But his character would have to change; he would have to become a Charlie (a tramp clown) instead of an acrobatic clown. He zealously studied books written in German about the art of mime. He read everything he could lay his hands on about clowns and actors. He studied psychology and read critiques of pantomime performances. He harked back to his early days in New York City, when he had spoken no English, and had been incensed at the laughter his attempts at communication had engendered. If he could create the same sort of laughter by bits of juggling and balancing stunts of little consequence, then become outraged at the minimal response, he would have developed a genuinely humorous routine out of his own remembered feelings. Furthermore, it had not been done before. Flat on his back, he taught himself to juggle and practiced facial reactions in a mirror.

After leaving the hospital, he played many circuses for a period of about twenty years, developing his art to a fine edge. At last, when his least gesture was incredibly calculated, and when he had learned the right time to perform a broad, gross routine as opposed to a subtle one, he joined Ringling Bros. Circus. That was in 1951. Except for a strike by the American Guild of Variety Artists that took Griebling briefly away to perform in a one-ring rival circus in Boston, Massachusetts, he had been with the show ever since.

When Emmett Kelly (who once worked Ringling together with Griebling) left the limelight, audiences realized that it was Griebling, not Kelly, who did the really heavy clowning back in those days. Before Griebling's arrival on the Ringling scene, the management of the show had called up the big guns of circus promotion and had entered into a calculated, prolonged buildup of the notable Kelly's "Willie" character. But it is to Griebling's credit that the dice rolled by fate decreed him to be paramount in his art. He worked long and hard at the development of his haughtily outraged characterization. He richly deserved his preeminence, as he equally deserved the accolade given him on that April 28. In point of fact he was the best there was.

It was during the 1970 stand at Madison Square Garden that I was talking with a group of Augustes at the back door as we watched Griebling work before the show started. Two of the clowns were with Ringling for their first year, though not in any sense novices in their profession. Since it was just after Griebling's birthday, someone on the staff had flippantly suggested that they take him out and "turn him on" with pot. The joke was greeted with icy calm on the part of those who heard it.

"To begin with," one said, "his voice box has been removed because of cancer. To suggest smoking in any form seems a little cruel, don't you think?"

"It sure does," another answered. "Anyway, why change what goes on in that head in the first place. If I had half the beautiful thoughts that Griebling does I wouldn't have to spend time studying what to do to make people laugh. My God, what a beautiful brain that guy has!"

We fell silent, watching the artist work the audience into a frenzy, preparing it for the beginning of the show. We all agreed that it was noteworthy for such a huge thing as Ringling Bros. Circus to rely on one man—one special man—to build enthusiasm in an audience, to adjust the mood of a massive crowd so that the circus could begin already ahead of the game. What we saw from behind the red-and-white-striped curtains was almost unbelievable. Every step that Griebling took was evocative of the tawdry character he portrayed. Even out of the spotlight, he bumbled along in those noxious, green, woolly slippers, seemingly oblivious to the fact that his character was a born loser.

"He is a driven man," said a voice behind me. "He doesn't have to do that. He has worked hard and saved all his life. He owns his own home, and he's in his seventies. There just isn't any other answer. He's driven."

"By what?" I wondered.

I needn't have. The roar that descended from the audience onto the little figure of a beat-up tramp, standing alone in the center ring, was more than answer enough.

After the show that day, a friend and I sat in a bar across from the Garden as the performance was letting out. Griebling wandered in and mouthed a request to the bartender. My friend recognized him at once, and said "Give that gentleman anything he wants." Griebling waved his hand and shook his head no. The bartender couldn't understand him, and asked for a repetition. Annoyed after performing in two shows that day, Griebling gestured for a pencil, and wrote his request on a napkin. The bartender couldn't make it out, and consulted us. It said, "Three bottles 7UP." The bartender refused him, because bottles of any kind cannot be sold across the bar in the city by law. Griebling shrugged, waved goodbye to us in an offhand and genuinely funny gesture, and padded off.

"Who's that?" the bartender wanted to know. "Probably the greatest clown in the world," my friend answered. I couldn't have agreed more.

staten island
REGISTER

OBITUARIES

The day that laughter died

On April 19, 1972 the sound of laughter died in St. Clare's Hospital, New York City. Though the circus clowns raced madly on their frenzied ways, the soul of the circus, the greatest clown of his type anywhere in the world today, Otto Griebling died.

Griebling was a satirist, rather than a cartoon as are most clowns today. He was at loggerheads with society around him—a world that consistently passed him by as if it was too busy to notice the scruffy little bag of a man belligerently demanding attention. He was beautiful.

I had fallen into a habit of purchasing a six pack of 7-Up for him every April 28, for that was his birthday. On opening night of the circus here in New York this year I saw him standing in the wing, and went to tell him that his beverage would be around as usual. Otto curtseyed, as if to royalty in response, because he had been voiceless for some time now, a victim of cancer of the throat. I pointed out the place where my friends and I were sitting, and before the show began he came along the hippodrome in front of us. He performed a little routine, balancing a pie plate on his nose then

curtsying again. After that he went on to the center ring, where he gave a brilliant rendition of his famous pre-performance warm-up routine that delighted the entire audience at Madison Square Garden.

It was a great performance, and, it turned out, it was his last. Now it seems as if clowns aren't that funny anymore, at least not to me.

One of the many components that combine to make a good clown great is his makeup, or "face" as it is called. But I have always felt that the face beneath the face is as important as the decoration that makes the face a clown. Kelly's makeup was unique and delicately shaded from one hue to another. It was a masterpiece in the same sense that some Japanese theatrical makeup is especially successful. It was, among other things, subtle. Griebling's was far less so—an intentional difference that was entirely fitting for the difference in character between the two clowns. The great performing clown of Russia, Popov, uses little makeup. His face so naturally embodies wide-eyed innocence with a touch of slyness that makeup is not needed.

In most cases, good clown makeup is an extension, or enlargement, of facial characteristics that already exist. Furrows from nose to mouth are darkened, or crinkles at the edge of the eyes are made more prominent so that they can be utilized during reactive grimaces when the performer is in the ring.

Of the whiteface clowns, one of the more interesting is the great Lou Jacobs, whose extreme makeup takes as long as a half hour to put on. His slapstick and broad gestures are perfectly suited to the massive arenas in which the Ringling circus plays. His elongated head, topped by a ridiculous little hat, is plastered with enormous eyebrows on its forehead. The rubber ball nose that he uses is a Jacobs trademark, no matter who else uses it. His lips, broadly etched in a smile that nearly reaches his ears, can be seen in the most distant reaches of any arena. Thus, when he comes onto the hippodrome track, everyone knows who he is. He may appear in female attire—a huge, plumed hat atop his head and a purple evening dress over his slinking frame as he leads his St. Bernard-sized Dachshunds around the ring, or carries a delightful little mutt named Knucklehead on the train of his dress—but everybody knows who it is by the makeup. Jacobs is one of the few clowns who has been allotted a lengthy solo of his own in the center ring. This is his inspired routine involving a miniscule automobile. The sight of such

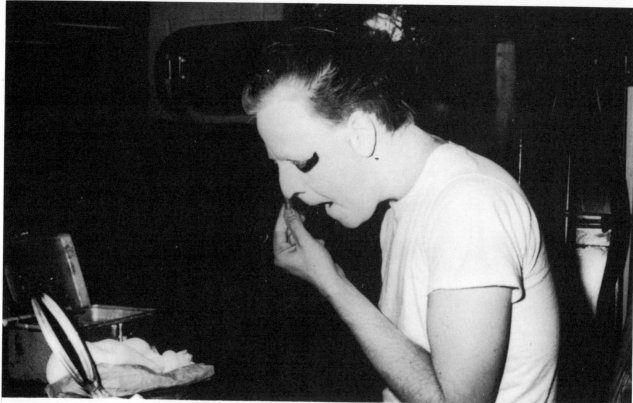

After putting on a white base, "Sparky" applies color to his nose.

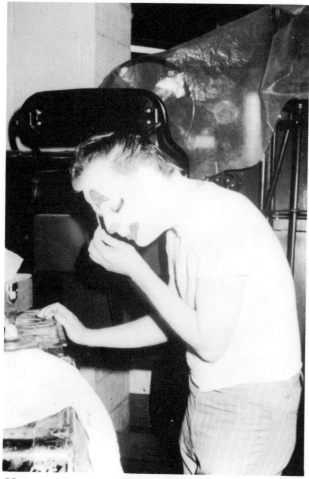

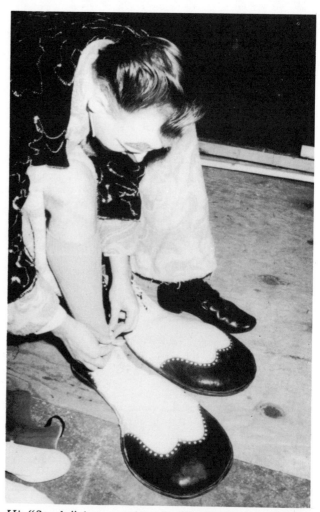

Next comes black lining for sequin-dusted eyebrows.

His "Sparky" face complete, D. W. Washburn takes care of his costume, including enormous flap shoes.

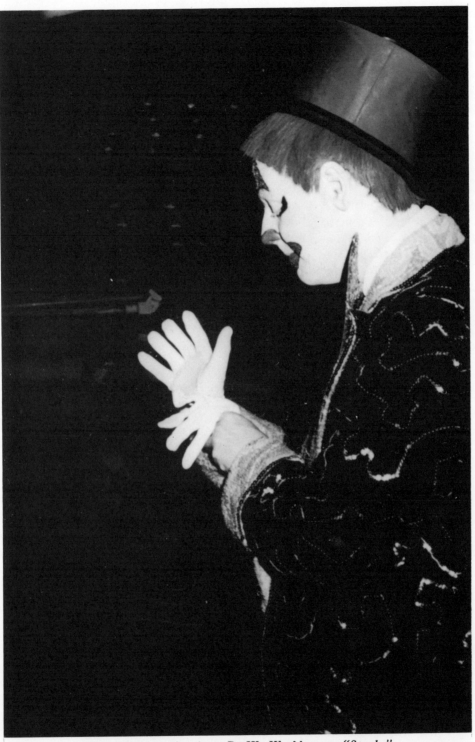

The transformation from D. W. Washburn to "Sparky"
being complete, the clown dons immaculate, white gloves
as he readies himself for an appearance in the ring.

a large man as Jacobs emerging from that tiny car is enough to tickle the fancy of many a circus-goer. The disembarking is made all the more preposterous by the manner in which it is done. The little door swings open. An enormous foot, half the size of the car itself, is slowly thrust high in the air from the cab, where it flaps up and down on the end of a long leg. Next a head appears. Then a hand, which removes the hat from the head to wave it at the audience. By this time, the leg, arm, and head completely fill the tiny doorway of the car. With enormous effort, more Jacobs emerges until the full height of the man towers above the automobile. This introduction to the act unfailingly brings the house down. Though there have been more than a few imitations of Jacobs (clowns steal material from one another persistently), none have touched his routine with the midget car for the simple reason that none except Jacobs happens to be both a mechanic and a contortionist at the same time. If they did possess these skills, they would also need the dash of genius owned by Jacobs; and such a weird combination of skills and talent is not easy to come by.

If there is one clown that I ever wished to see, that clown was Grock. His is the name that comes to every European mind when the word clown is spoken. Written accounts (including his own) have so remarkably captured the essence of Grock, and so well revealed his inspired genius, that I can talk about Grock as if I, myself, had witnessed his famous routines.

Picture him fumbling onstage (or into the ring) in his huge overcoat. His head, made up to emphasize his large jaw, was covered by a skullcap similar to a roof with its eaves protruding over his ears. His black string tie fastened his white shirt together, and his boots stuck out under his overcoat. He carried a cello case onstage with him. Searching diligently inside it, he came up with a fiddle. Full of assurance, Grock placed the fiddle under his chin and gave the bow a spin in the air—

as if he had always performed this rite before playing for an audience. Absentmindedly, he held his hand out to catch the bow, but it fell clattering to the floor. Annoyed, he picked it up and tossed it skywards again. Again he missed. He repeated these attempts several times, then shamefully retreated behind a boudoir screen. Desperate flights of the bow above the screen, followed by the sound of the bow clattering on the floor, informed the audience that Grock was manfully trying to master this preperformance flourish. It was all to no avail. Finally Grock emerged from behind the screen, apparently to begin playing and to eliminate the trick of tossing the bow in the air; but he absentmindedly threw it up anyway, more out of force of habit than anything else. As it fell earthward he unconsciously caught it. With a masterful doubletake, Grock realized what he had done and bellowed his pleasure at the now hysterical audience!

Such inspired bits of clowning take months of minute attention to detail, and years of character study to develop. It is quite true that being funny is a serious business. It seems equally true that the long, solo episodes performed by European clowns and hinted at by the shorter solo acts involving the great American "warmup" clowns, are destined to disappear from the circus scene. The pace and schedule of a large, modern circus does not allow for much character development onstage. These days, the character must be full-blown from the start. Spectators are no longer allowed the luxury of watching a character develop through a series of foibles.

By allowing pace and precision to eclipse the slow development of a clown's character, our gigantic circuses hand this unique and characteristic feature to smaller road shows, much to the delight of purists, who claim that the true spirit of the circus in America remains, in the 1970s, under canvas, still.

14
ONE-HUMPED CURIOS

DIFFERING FROM ALL other mammals in the shape of their red blood corpuscles are members of the camel family; an interesting but not important fact, in my opinion. Far more important to me is that camels differ from other mammals because of their pungent, permeating odor, which is noxious.

There are members of the camel family living in both hemispheres. Dromedaries, or one-humped camels, are from Africa, and Bactrian, or two-humped camels, are from Asia. Other members are the vicuna, alpaca, guanaco, and llama (all from South America).

Virtually a legend as a beast of burden in desert areas, the camel is well adapted to such a rigorous environment. It has prominent knee pads, the better to fit its habit of reposing with its front feet folded beneath it, and broad, padlike feet, the better to carry it across sandy soil.

When rising to a standing position after having been loaded with desert freight, the camel first hefts its hind legs up while remaining on its front knees. Then it laboriously drags its weight to a standing position by raising one foreleg after another, complaining loudly as it does so.

The hair is well developed on the humps, head, neck, and "forearms" of both types of camel. Like cows, they possess three-chambered stomachs. The gestation period is from 370 to 440 days, after which one young is born. The birth of twins occurs only rarely.

The term "ship of the desert" is due partly to the camel's being the principal means of transport in that area, and partly to the rolling motion un-dertaken by the beast when it walks or runs. This motion results in a violent, pelvic lurch for the camel's rider. As soon as he recovers from the initial jarring, he is thrown into a second one, as the other side of the camel dips when the feet on that side step forward in unison.

Life in the desert is harsh, and both the people and the animals that succeed in living there are hardened beings. The camel has helped man to survive under these conditions by providing him with many aids for survival. In addition to being a hardy beast of burden, it supplies milk and meat, wool, hides, sinews, and bones. Chemicals are even extracted from its dung and urine.

The camel itself survives by being able to eat plants that no other herbivore can or will devour. If these are scarce, a camel will eat fish, meat, bones, and skin. It can and does thrive on brackish or salt water.

As a guard against driving sandstorms, the camel's ears are haired on the inside. It possesses long, heavy eyelashes and its nostrils are closable. A groove extends from each nostril to the animal's lip, thereby allowing the beast to catch any moisture that runs from its nose; on the desert an ounce of moisture can save a life.

A camel in good health has its humps erect, whereas, if it has been insufficiently fed, the humps will lean to one side or the other. But the main loss of moisture on the desert is from sweat, and in this our odoriferous friend has far more insurance than does man; the skin of this enormous and cantankerous beast has almost no sweat glands at all.

A circus camel obligingly poses beside the workers' sleeping van.

There has long been a question concerning the camels ridden by the Wise Men at the time of Christ's birth. Some argue that since Jerusalem is in Africa, the camels must surely have been dromedaries. Others argue that the kings were, in fact, Eastern potentates; therefore the camels must have been Bactrians. This point of difference is obvious even in the little nativity sets sold before the Christmas holiday season. Some manufacturers produce one-humped, while others produce two-humped camels!

Never mind. The point is clear that, if the Wise Men rode camels to travel so far, they chose wisely indeed, for, on the desert, camel transport is the surest way of getting there.

My curiosity about camels led me to seek out the foremost American trainer of camels, at Ringling Bros. Circus, where, on my way, I skirted three of the beasts tethered in the menagerie. I was looking for Jack Joyce whose camel act was with the show. Giving the baleful animals a wide

berth (they looked suspiciously at me, I felt) I met a beleaguered Mr. Joyce in a tiny show office, where he had briefly retired to catch his wind between his duties in the arena. With a few words sandwiched between many interruptions, I learned something of Mr. Joyce's history as a camel trainer.

He started in this unique enterprise when he was called to Australia in 1947 to train horses for an Australian circus. At that time camels could not be imported into America from Africa because of the threat of hoof-and-mouth disease to American livestock. Mr. Joyce discovered that the camels in Australia were considered "clean" as far as the American government was concerned. Camels had once been imported for transport duty on the Australian desert, and the animals that Joyce discovered were descendants of those original beasts, running semiwild on the vast expanses of Australia's huge ranches.

He brought twenty camels back with him, and shrewdly picked as many pregnant females as he

A King Bros. camel balefully surveys the lot.

seems to be that camels are the only animals in the world that refuse to speak to each other. They dislike each other heartily. But Joyce has found that camels, although slow to catch on, respond well to patient and carefully planned handling. Once they learn something, he considers them about on a par with horses. They are by temperament more defensive than equines and bite or kick more readily when they think that they must defend themselves. Joyce claims that they are more deliberate than horses, and often lazier, but he feels that laziness is an individual characteristic.

"Camels are, after all, one of the oldest domesticated animals in the world," Joyce added.

"How would you rate them as far as general

could. Since there had never been a successful camel act, he "broke one in" (i.e. trained, or created one) in 1950.

The camels perform an act similar to that presented by liberty horses in the ring, adding to the presentation the strangeness of their lope, giving their amblings a floating appearance. The act, which also included llamas, was a sensation. It played Shrine circuses, state fairs, and was the first big animal act to perform on television's "Ed Sullivan Show."

"We came back to the 'Sullivan Show' three times," Joyce said, refusing my offer of a cigarette and pulling from his pocket a package of—you guessed it—Camels.

Joyce has read a great deal about camels, and claims that the bulk of camel information exists in British publications, owing to the long stay of British forces in North Africa. The British view

A King Bros. camel settles down to await the erection of the menagerie tent. Like most camels, it would prefer waiting to actually doing anything.

intelligence goes?" I was aware, when I asked this question, that I was asking for volumes of information.

"Well," Joyce inhaled the smoke from his cigarette and smiled slightly, revealing that he knew the enormity of the question. "To tell the truth, they're pretty damned intelligent. Maybe shrewd would be a better word. I mean, they sure won't kill themselves working, like a jackass will. You've got to admit, that's pretty shrewd!"

Joyce exhibits his camels together with llamas, ponies, and zebras—the latter of which are the most difficult because of their two instinctive reactions, kicking and running. Zebras are hunted animals and know it, according to Joyce. They are the only truly wild animals in his routine.

"What do you look for in a camel that you are going to buy for your act?" I asked.

"Well, the training is up to you, so what you look for is the best-appearing specimen of its type, and one that's not too old. But the most important thing, I think, is beauty."

Somewhat stunned by this answer, I thanked Joyce for the time he had given me in his frantically busy schedule, and we parted company.

But I shook my head in wonder as I walked past those three, towering, gawky, and odoriferous beasts in the menagerie. Beauty? In a camel? I suppose it all depends on your point of view. But I still wonder how anyone can see beauty in a thing like that!

15

THE SPOTTED SAVAGE

THE HABITAT RANGE of leopards is the largest of any big cat. Their population extends practically all over Africa with the exception of the Sahara, although the animals are becoming rare in North Africa, and in the more populated areas of South Africa as well. They are, like so many animals beautiful enough to be "appreciated" by man, declining in numbers rapidly. In Asia, leopards are found from China in the west to Japan in the east, and in Southeast Asia they are found in India and Indonesia, together with its islands.

Among scientists (who presume to tell us what is what) the subspecies, based on regional variations, include many types of leopards. But for all practical purposes there is remarkably little difference between specimens from different areas, with the exception of a dramatic example like *Panthera pardus japonensis* from northern China, whose rosettelike spots are unusually large, and whose fur is much longer than is common among leopards.

Leopards are mostly nocturnal, and are particularly shy and secretive. This, however, is in no way indicative of a gentle nature. They are famed for their savagery, which one authority claims to be unequalled by any wild animal. They and cunning and possess such quick reflexes that their presence strikes instant fear in the hearts of humans who live in the vicinity when those animals are on the prowl. The same is apparently felt by small mammals and birds that happen to be within the borders of a leopard's territory. As the spotted savage glides silently through the heavy cover that is his domain, rendered all but invisible by the night's darkness and his broken pattern, he is surrounded by a tense and eerie vacuum of silence, pregnant with the feeling of an event about to occur. It usually does. Daytime prowling differs little, for the leopard is a master at camouflage. Few can actually see him. Most that do, do so for a short time only, because they are marked as prey.

Although few texts deal with the subject, odor undoubtedly plays a part in the hunting techniques of the leopard. It is easy to imagine a monkey, quiet with fear at the approach of a leopard on the ground below, panic inwardly as the cat comes close. Such a feeling produces the same, increased flow of adrenalin in a monkey as it does in humans. The result is an increase in body odor—instantly recognizable to a predator like the leopard, whose every sense is so acutely tuned that the least variation in conditions around him is a signal.

If all of the foregoing description can be attributed to the spotted savage, it can be doubled if applied to the black leopard, according to legend. This animal, which is not really black at all, but actually a blackish, charcoal brown, is considered by many to be the personification of malevolence. But as far as I can determine, the black leopard is in no way different from the spotted. It is not a different species, and is often born in a mixed litter. Nevertheless, it occurs most commonly in India and Southeast Asia, in the most humid area of the leopard's range. The black leopard may survive because of its excellent camouflage, considering the fact that nightly prowls are its habit. On the other hand, its camouflage during the daylight hours is notably poor. It is actually spotted, as can be seen when strong sunlight strikes its fur at the proper angle.

The black leopard is often referred to as a black panther, a term used locally to designate several of the wild cats. (Pumas, or cougars, as well as the black jaguar, are also called "panthers" in certain areas.) But it should be understood that no such animal as a panther exists as a scientific classification of any feline.

Black or spotted, leopards can and do become relatively tractable in captivity—or perhaps I should say *some* leopards, for again the policy of treating any animal type as a group fails. Like all living creatures, leopards are individuals. I once met one at an animal farm in New Jersey and was shocked to hear the proprietor ask if I would like him to take the animal out so that I could pose for pictures. I agreed, and spent a shaky fifteen minutes posing in the yard with the adult animal restrained by nothing more than a frayed piece of clothesline. Later, when in charge of cats at a zoo, an aged, spotted male and I became fast friends. His condition on arrival was decrepit enough to make other members of the staff dislike him. Perhaps for this reason, he responded strongly to my friendliness, and in short order allowed me to rub his ears, scratch beneath his chin, and even place my fingers in his mouth. Zukka, as he was called, craved affection and attention in surroundings that were new, strange, and hostile to him. Unable to digest slabs of horsemeat at first, he greedily devoured the same meat when it was ground, and often ate it from my outstretched palm, much to the consternation of observers. Although charging the bars with all of the ferocity expected from a leopard, the touch of his mouth on my hand was like a feather, and he took the meat in little nibbles from me. When eating from the floor of his cage, his actions were different. In that situation he licked the food into his mouth, after a few, preliminary gulps, with a great deal of force. Obviously, he knew the difference.

At the same zoo, I cared for a pair of exceptionally savage and aggressive black leopards. The female, Shiva, was in her prime and a nearly perfect example of her type. Never a day passed that didn't allow a moment for my appreciation of her beauty. But trying to "reach" her, to establish a rapport, was nearly impossible. Virtually every attempt at establishing a bond was met with failure. After some months, she held her ferocity in check enough to permit me to stroke her nose lightly with a short stick as she rolled onto her back, but she continued to utter throaty growls as she did so. The slightest variation in the routine, such as the shifting of my weight outside the cage, immediately sent her into spasms of anger. When such a distracting influence occurred, she spun to her feet, flung herself at the bars and spat convulsively into my face, inches away. I never observed the entire action at one time, so great was her speed, and was grateful that the cage bars were spaced so that she could not reach out further than six inches.

Although I was pleased that we had progressed as far as we had in the establishment of a tolerable association between us, I never really trusted her. It seemed to me that she desperately craved rapport with her keeper, and wanted equally to offer it in return; but it also seemed that she could not do so because she was a leopard. (After all, she had to maintain her reputation at all cost!)

Shiva, bless her little black heart, was responsible for the only incapacitating injury that I have received from a wild member of the cat family to date.

It happened two days before Christmas in 1970. Shiva was in a cage with her two cubs, one spotted and one black. During the times when she cared for her young, she was even more vicious than usual. Until that day the cubs had remained in the den, outside the cage itself and ineffectively insulated against the winter cold. The den's entrance opened into the rear of the inside cage in the animal building. Owing to a temperature drop, the cubs found it more comfortable to remain in the cage, rather than the den, and in full view of zoo visitors. This made Shiva terribly upset. When I passed her cage, she sprang at the bars, snarling and spitting. Repeatedly, she gathered her cubs in her mouth and carried them back into the den, only to have them wander out into the cage again, much to her consternation.

Feeding time presented special problems with the cubs underfoot. As I approached the cage Shiva sprang again and again at the bars, beside herself with panic, but desperately hungry at the same time. Coming abreast of the cage, I saw that between Shiva and the bars sat the little spotted cub, directly in Shiva's way as she grabbed for the meat. Thinking that I should give her a chance to move her cub aside, I bypassed the cage and fed the jaguar housed next to her. Glancing back at the leopard cage, I saw that Shiva had knocked her cub aside and was now directly at the bars, spitting and salivating in anticipation of her dinner.

The noise and confusion of the feeding operation had drawn schoolchildren to the area, accompanied by their teachers. The crowd stood uncomfortably close behind me. One of the teachers was directly to my rear.

I extended the meat in my right hand, swinging it so that Shiva could catch the free end as it slid between the bars. This process of hand feeding is not one that zoos everywhere endorse. The keeping staff had developed it in order to come as close to actual contact as possible with the various members of our captive group of cats. In this way we would each learn about one another, and hasten the establishment of the animal-keeper bond that is the mark of good animal-keeping.

Shiva missed the meat on its first swing through the bars. I grabbed the meat with both hands and extended it closer to the bars with my left hand, an action that I performed many times before and after the accident, without injury.

At that point a teacher behind me asked, "Isn't that dangerous?"

Precisely at that instant I made my mistake. I paid attention to her, and turned my head slightly in her direction to answer her. My intentions were to tell her that it was indeed dangerous, and that she shouldn't talk with me while I was feeding the animals. I never got the chance.

Shiva, frenzied by hunger, snagged her claw into the inside of the middle finger of my left hand, drove it at once to the bone, and started to pull the hand into the cage. The injury was without pain, as she immediately severed the nerve endings close to the skin. Scarcely willing to offer my hand for her lunch, I yanked it quickly backward. So, in a sense, it was I, rather than the cat, who made the injury as incapacitating as it turned out to be.

I had always devoted considerable time in my zoo work to the explanation of exactly why a visitor should never talk to a keeper while he is at work with an animal. At the time of the accident, I was reminded how far theory is from practice!

There is something of a lesson in this tale. If you visit with a keeper at the zoo while he is feeding his animals, don't assume that he is giving you a cold shoulder out of personal distaste if he ignores your questions. In my opinion, you do not have the right to ask them in the first place. Not at feeding time, anyway.

Black or otherwise, leopards are less common than lions or tigers as performers. They are smaller than those cats, and do not present as formida- ble, or "death defying" an appearance in America's arenas, although they are, in fact, much more dangerous to present. Few trainers choose to pit themselves against the speed and treachery of leopards, especially since they are aware that audiences do not respond to them as dramatically as they do to the larger cats.

To find a genuinely great presentation of leopards in the ring we must go back to the 1940s when a gentle, aristocratic Frenchman by the name of Alfred Court, who had come to America fleeing the Nazis (together with no less than eighty cats) and took circus audiences in the United States by storm when he presented three rings of wild animals, aided by two trainers under his tutelage. The Court appearances in Ringling Bros. Circus left spectators thunderstruck, for they were far different from anything witnessed previously in America. Basing his presentation on the formation of exotic tableaux with mixed groups of wild cats, dogs, and bears, Court left audiences gasping at the climax of each pyramid formation. In each ring the animals mounted pedestals, the tops of which concealed powerful spotlights directed upwards. At a given signal, the arena was plunged into total darkness and three rings full of spotlighted pedestals were switched on as the animals atop them simultaneously rose on their haunches to a sitting position. Spotted and black leopards, together with pumas, were featured by Court in the center ring, and later by his Hindu protégé, Damoo Dohtre, in an end ring.

From this spectacular debut, where could Court go to improve the presentation for another year? How could the act be made even more appealing? It seemed that he had reached the ultimate already.

But no. Court could and did produce a new act that was an immediate success. Shunting unwanted animals to the end rings, he created a center-ring animal act that consisted of twelve, spotted leopards—and twelve girls!

The showgirls did not appear on the scene until the act had been perfected with the temporary use of cage boys and helpers (dressed in pink tights!). Handing the actual training of the leopards over to an assistant at this point, Court personally escorted each girl into the ring and guided her next to the man whose place she would eventually fill. The girls were instructed to pay no attention to the leopards whatsoever, for that was Court's job. Though steel-nerved, the girls always were a trifle shaky in the ring, as they posed together with the leopards in the pyramids. In the culminating routine two of the girls held a third over their heads horizontally, while a beautiful leopard leaped over her to a seat on a high pedestal some distance away. (I can remember how she winced as that furry, murderous animal grazed her bare midriff while she was held aloft, and wonder if the girls drew lots for the privilege —with the loser assigned to it!)

The act's appearance was, of course, an immediate hit. Billed as "Beauties and the Beasts," it made much of the fact that the true wonder did not exist in the routines performed at all, but in the totally incongruous mixture of participants. In each leopard's head was a mind that constantly wandered, constantly schemed, and constantly reacted to the slightest distraction. That same mind was anxiously awaiting the chance to trigger reflex actions and energies so supersonic in speed that it was nearly impossible to stop them. Every one of those twelve minds, strung taut by the excitement around them, was compelled by a force emanating from their trainer to yield *total* attention to Alfred Court himself. It was a study in relationship between man and beast, and an example of training and rapport that Americans would not see again for a quarter of a century.

But in 1971 I ran into such an act. It consisted of spotted and black leopards, and was trained by Dick Chipperfield, one of the directors of the famed English circus. It was an effective and curious animal act at Madison Square Garden, where Ringling Bros. Circus was appearing.

I say that the act was "curious" because it was performed so casually and easily that it didn't appear to be a difficult achievement at all. This is quite the reverse of the actual situation.

According to Chipperfield, the main difficulty in training cats is that it takes longer. He explained this during an interview between circus performances.

"Leopards, you see, are even more loners than tigers. Among leopards themselves, those that are black have the reputation of being more solitary than their spotted cousins, perhaps because there are fewer of them. They tend to stick to themselves, and it is generally thought that they even go so far as to stick with one mate, where spotted leopards are more polygamous, you might say."

Although this sounded reasonable enough, it gave rise to questions concerning the leopards in his act.

"How come, if they are considered solitary animals, you not only toss them and carry them around, let them lie down on top of you and jump into your arms, but you also let both spotted and black live together?" I asked.

"Two reasons explain this," Chipperfield said, yawning from the exhaustion of a three-performance Saturday. "First, with leopards I like to get them very young. They were all babies together—all except one, that I broke in a little later than the rest—and they don't know anything else except to live together. Another reason is concealed in what I told you earlier—it takes longer to train leopards. This is because complete trust must be built up in them. They must know that whatever I ask them to do will not harm them.

"I got them when they were three months old, and kept them together so that they relied on each other for security. That took care of the problem of mixing the two color phases. But I didn't start training them until about ten months. When they are that old, they have some thinking apparatus working for them, and are not easily distracted. Trying to teach a baby leopard is just like trying to teach a four-month-old baby to talk."

I observed that the variety of stunts performed by Chipperfield leopards was unusual. Aside from the various striking tableaux that they form, pyramid style, they perform beautiful leaps over Chipperfield's head, and through a very small hoop. At the close of the act, a black leopard leaps from a high stool, sailing through the air with its forelimbs extended to land directly on Chipperfield's chest, where it is forthwith embraced in a bear hug by the trainer, slapped on the rump, and scooted out of the arena. This is an amazingly dangerous feat to perform with an animal like a leopard, which is naturally high-strung and nervous. Following a leap, its natural instinct would be to kill, and its front paws and mouth are at precisely the correct position to do this—directly at Chipperfield's throat. In a still more remarkable display of confidence in his charges, Chipperfield lies prone on the arena floor while four leopards, two black and two spotted, sneak up to him and lie, side by side, across his body. Here the trainer is completely defenseless, without aids of any sort, and must literally hope for the best if the animals quarrel among themselves. (They did so when I watched the act, but were quieted by a pat and a stroke from their supine trainer.) My reaction, after having witnessed the routine, was to ask Chipperfield how he decided on which trick to teach which leopard.

"That's kind of an interesting question, you

Chipperfield, smothered by leopards.

Chipperfield's black leopard soars through a hoop.

know. Actually, with a bunch of leopards all together, you don't decide on a trick and then teach them to do it. You watch them, and learn what their aptitudes are, and build from that. They show you what they want to do first; then you take it from there. Some leopards love to be carried when they are youngsters; so I develop those into the ones I can wear around my neck like a collar, or carry upside down in my arms. Others like to leap, and there are lots of routines one can develop from that."

"Your act is so quiet, so simple in the way you do it, that it doesn't seem like the enormous feat that it really is," I said.

"Ah, now you sound like an American," he said, grinning broadly. "Why should it seem otherwise? If it's action and roars you want, you can always watch my lion act. But I'm not trying to impress the public with *my* abilities. I am trying to show them how smart my pupils are. Sure, they're dangerous. Everybody knows that already. But I want them to learn how smart they are, and how beautiful. A leopard leaping beats a lion all hollow, you know. And leopards performing together represent much more of an achievement than lions, because lions live together anyway."

"Are your animals individually named?"

"Of course."

"Can you rattle them off the top of your head?"

"O Lord, now let's see—Sari, Anyi, Mowgli, Bendhira, Chota, Sindi, Chira, and Engwe. They're all Indian names except for Engwe, which is African. It's Zulu for leopard."

"Do you plan to introduce any more specimens into the act?"

"Not here. But I've got a bunch of cubs back there, so it seems to me that it would only be natural to add them until I have a large group to present—particularly if I am going to present them here in America, in your huge arenas."

"Only natural" are the key words in Chipperfield's last statement, for his animals perform feats that are extensions of their natural abilities, and his association with them in the ring seems, in fact, "only natural."

Our conversation turned to other trainers, then to circus life in general. While I listened to Chipperfield's meandering conversation, I studied him as we sat in the trailer. He was visibly tired from the performance of not only his leopard act, but from the showing of his blustery, nine-lion act only minutes later. Feeling that I had grasped the human-animal relationship at work in the Chipperfield leopard act, I finished the beer that he had offered me and said my goodbyes.

"Cheerio," Chipperfield said. Then, almost without pause, he turned to his cage man and asked him to help move cages into a better position, and to remove the cracker from the whip, replacing it with a certain bit of green leather that Chipperfield found more effective. The pause for the interview had so relaxed him that it had made him drowsy; once back into the swing of things, he galvanized into action.

Walking away, I wondered where animal trainers get their energy. One minute they seem to be dead on their feet, and the next bursting with activity. I wondered if they catnapped, like their charges; but I don't suppose that I shall ever be certain. I was convinced of only one thing—that Chipperfield gave every ounce of his energies, every bit of his concentration to his career. His black and spotted leopards were the very cause for his existence. Their sinewy, steel-muscled forms virtually seemed to entrap the remarkable trainer's soul, to fuse him with his savages until they thought, acted, and felt as one.

It was Chipperfield who convinced me that this oneness is the hallmark of truly great animal training, and it was a realization as beautiful as it was astounding.

Ringling's 100th Anniversary spec was brilliantly conceived and produced.

Exhaustion prompts a candid pose of wearisome tranquility by an anonymous Ringling clown.

Clad in gypsy attire show girls, grooms, and Hugo Schmitt parade around the hippodrome track for the presentation of the elephant act.

Billy and Dinah Stephenson, here shown as the Riding Saxons, check performance details before starting the act.

16
WATCHMAN BY DEFAULT
(A BACKYARD IMPRESSION)

EARLY IN JUNE, 1971, I visited my friends at Circus Bartok when the show played Bayonne, New Jersey. As with most of my circus visits, I arrived early in the morning in order to spend a full day on the lot. Roland Kaiser, operator of the show's front end (the concessions and side show that usually form a walkway to the entrance of the big show) saw to it that I was given a two-day pass to the cookhouse, and promised me a bunk for the night. Bunni Bartok and Jan Perz, a married team of producer and manager, were not yet up, nor were Doc and Betty Bartok, the show's owners. I sat over coffee, "jackpotting" (gossiping) with Roland and a young clown named Phil, also an early riser. Interest was high concerning a night off, for the evening show was at 6:30, and the remainder of the night was free. Freedom in such close proximity to New York City is always greeted with anticipation. Long confined to life on the lot, performers and workmen all yearn for a chance to kick up their heels in a city as large as Manhattan, although I who lived in New York welcomed the chance to spend time in the open-air "rurality" of a circus lot.

Meeting those with whom I had struck up an acquaintance in previous years was a pleasure. Some, who had met me when I had visited the show's winter quarters during the previous season, were even more open in their greetings; I began to understand the feeling between people who meet while on tour. It seems to represent a touching of kindred souls, a visit from another person who is

"with it." It is an event among meetings with hundreds of individuals who are foreigners or "towners," and it makes one feel unusually warm when it occurs.

I caught sight of Bunni and Jan across the lot, and walked towards them. During my trip, Bunni re-entered the trailer and Jan went off on other business. I advanced toward the trailer, aware that it was guarded by an enormous, white police dog by the name of Mruz (Polish for blizzard).

Before I could mention his name, the dog emerged from beneath the trailer as if to attack me, like he did with all comers. Suddenly he stopped short. His tail began a tentative wag. My touch brought his wagging apparatus into full play, and his greeting to me was ecstatic.

To a "towner" like myself, thrilled when recognized by the humblest circus personality, the greeting and recognition by that enormous and beautiful dog was impressive.

Great indecision persisted among circus personnel concerning what they would do "on their night off." Jan insisted that he would not go anywhere, but would go immediately to sleep because he was bone tired. Bunni had wanted to take the children "in town" for a supervised sample of high life, but decided to yield to Jan's wishes. Doc and Betty were expecting visitors.

Such is the extemporaneous nature of off-duty circus life, that Jan received a visitor early in the evening. A Polish friend, he sat with Jan and myself, jabbering away in his native tongue, offering me more and more liquor and continuously apologizing for talking in Polish. Entranced with the sound of it all, I merely urged the two onward, while feeling the effects of alcohol lacing through my body.

Word was sent from Doc and Betty's trailer that their company had arrived, and that they would all like me to drop in. Spotting a chance to get the bottle out of the trailer, Bunni handed it to me and mumbled something that I didn't fully hear, ushering me out of the door. Pausing to offer a nip to Mruz (who refused it) I bumbled my way to the owners' portable living quarters, and met the guests.

I cannot remember how the visit ended, except that somehow the liquor was gone, and we were outside the trailer again. Bunni was now calling upon me to prevent Jan from driving his Polish friend home. Sober enough to realize that such a drive would indeed be a dangerous undertaking for my friend, I ran to the driver's side of the truck and hung onto the door, pleading with him not to leave. Meanwhile, Bunni had secured the services of a sober worker named Tree (names like that are not unusual in a circus, although workers like that are, for Tree was a man of total reliability and constant good humor) who took over the driving, much to the relief of everyone.

At this point, Ryzard entered the scene. A hand balancer in the performance, he was in charge of three elephants: Jumbo, of customary size, and Betty and Bunny, two babies recently purchased. He came to talk about what should be done with the elephants, since the show was to be virtually deserted for the night. It was decided that the babies would be returned to the van in which they traveled, and that the adult could either be left outside or in the menagerie tent.

Doc and Betty retired, as did Bunni. Jan left with his Polish friend to visit a local Polish-American club.

Suddenly left without cohorts, I walked towards the menagerie, where I held up the sidewall while Ryzard led the baby elephants through its opening to the van. Following that, we returned together to the menagerie tent, where we stood for some two hours before Jumbo, talking to her and chatting about Ryzard's life with the circus. Ryzard talked at great length about his personal life, his marital troubles, and the need to find "someone right" to live with forever before one made the choice. His heavily accented conversation left no question about his devotion to the Bartoks, and his feelings about being accepted as a member of the family. Although I had seen him many times in the ring, I now felt a personal sympathy beginning to stir, as I realized the uncommon hardship of his existence. The pay was surely no more than adequate, but it included freedom—and it included being drawn into a family. What such an annexation must mean to a person like Ryzard can only be understood by someone who has gone through his own, particular experiences.

As we finally parted company, at about two in the morning, I began to look around for a place to sleep. I located the sleeping van belonging to concession workers and some of the clowns. Thinking that the uppermost bunk, next to the metal roof, would surely be unoccupied, I clambered up to it and fell asleep.

Around three o'clock, I was awakened by a series of inquisitive punches. A strange voice said to me, "Sombody's in mah buuuunk up heah!"

I mumbled something noncommital, only to hear the phrase repeated.

It was a concessionaire named "Rosie," who had been disturbed at finding an underwear-clad figure in *his* bunk. But the figure, awakened, grumbled that somebody was in *his* bunk. That somebody turned out to be me, and I was forthwith provided a sleeping place towards the door of the trailer. Thus rearranged, everybody went to sleep, with the exception of myself.

A loud crack startled me into full wakefulness. I lay in the bunk, listening for the sound again, and wondering what it could possibly be. Again I heard it, this time accompanied by a slight tearing noise. I couldn't resist investigation, and got up.

Emerging from the trailer at about three-thirty in the morning, I came upon an eerie and beautiful scene. A night chill had settled on the lot. Periodic clankings of chains that restrained animals were the only sounds to be heard. The big top hung limp, and covered with dew in the steel gray of the moonlight. A work light burned inside. I ducked beneath the sidewall to view a scene of total disarray. Aerial rigging hung over the single ring and swung idly in the eddies of night breezes, and the ground was littered with vast amounts of paper refuse, left from the evening performance of the night before. The show's organ, covered with a torn canvas, stood, spectrelike, at the performers entrance to the tent. In the distance a horse whinnied. Otherwise, a deadly silence had descended on the circus.

I was drawn as if by a magnet to the single ring. I walked around its curb, humming softly to myself tunes that were typical circus music. I looked up at the rigging and wondered if I dared climb it, but decided against it because it would be sure to awaken somebody with its squeaks and rattles. I sat on the curb and watched a large rat wander and shuffle through the papers on the ground. It was probably a water rat, for the show scarcely carried such parasites with it, and the lot was directly on the bay. The rodent spotted me, studied me for a moment, and wandered off in no particular hurry. At that moment, when I was alone in the tent, the entire circus was mine, in a magical sort of way.

A third "crack" pierced the air. It came from the menagerie tent, and I went to investigate it.

It was Jumbo. Resentful at being left alone in the tent, she had removed a quarter pole from the ground, and was waving its free end back and forth in her trunk. She studied me with beady eyes as I nervously approached.

Trying to think of appropriate commands, I could only come up with one. Although it didn't fit the situation, I decided to use it.

"Foot," I said.

Jumbo obligingly lifted one foot, as she did in the ring when she gave her salute, but she continued to wave the free end of the pole on her trunk with what I thought to be a menacing attitude.

"Nice Jumbo," I said, feeling like a fool.

I offered her the crushed remains of a chocolate bar from my pocket, hoping that she would put down the pole to take them in her trunk. She did in fact rest the base of the pole on the ground briefly. Taking the chocolate in her trunk, she deftly threw it into her mouth, wrapper and all, and quickly grabbed the pole again before I could reach it.

"Keep it, honey," I assured her as I left the tent to return to my bunk for the hour or two that remained of the night. I looked up at the top of the tent, where the pole's metal spike had been laced to the canvas itself. Surely, I thought, it wouldn't last much longer, and would be on the ground in the morning. There was nothing I could do.

I slept fitfully, dimly conscious of Jumbo with her king-sized club as I periodically awakened through the rest of the night. By six I was up. I checked the elephant again to discover that I was correct, for she now held the pole over her back, balancing it in a semidoze. Walking into the backyard, I observed that a llama was loose from its tether, and grazing calmly at the edge of the bay. I retrieved it and placed it alongside its cohorts in the backyard lineup of llamas, shetland ponies, and a zebra. Next, I observed a pony some half-mile distant, grazing on a baseball diamond. After several energetic attempts to catch it, I yielded and left it where it was. (Some time later I was non-plussed to see a local youth go directly to the pony, grasp its halter and bring it back to the lineup without difficulty.)

The early morning air was chilly and crisp. Assorted snores and grunts emerged from trailers, and a couple of recumbent forms slept soundly on the grass. Tethered animals stomped the ground and exhaled with snorting vigor as they stretched the dampness from their bodies. The menagerie tent wiggled suggestively, undoubtedly the product of Jumbo's elephantine skullduggery inside, but I decided not to investigate.

I was famished, but the cookhouse was empty, with a damp wind blowing through it. I ambled about the lot and watched the local citizens bring their dogs to the park for morning walks. They came close—but not too close—to the circus, curious at the novel livestock tethered on its grounds.

Filthy and starving, I wandered into the town in hopes of discovering an eatery that might be open, but Bayonne is sealed on Sunday morning. Even inquiries at the local firehouse brought no news of available coffee. With my bones aching, I walked for miles in an effort to find breakfast. Finally I returned to the lot around ten-thirty, still hungry.

At eleven, the cookhouse opened. Coffee that was undoubtedly terrible, but that tasted like ambrosia, was served by a groggy cook who tried to be pleasant about it, but who nonetheless failed miserably.

Shortly, scrambled eggs appeared. These together with bread, marmalade, and more coffee, comprised a breakfast that was unusually satisfying. More people appeared, and the morning sun seemed to brighten everyone's outlook as the tempo gradually picked up. Local children were hired, for the price of a pass, to sweep the interior of the big top, and souvenirs were prepared for sale at the afternoon show. Doc and Betty emerged from their trailer, looking bright and cheerful. Bunni arrived for breakfast, too, grumbling *sotto voce* to her mother, Betty, about the hour of Jan's return to the lot.

Sensing that Bunni didn't approve of liquor, I apologized for my mild inebriation the night before. Bunni gave me a disapproving scowl, then giggled. Everything was all right.

Although the impression given by life on the road is one of relative freedom, the confinement required by life with a show as small and close as Circus Bartok needs periodic breaking in order to keep the show loose enough for successful operation during the long season. One such break had occurred that night in Bayonne. It was right for Bunni and Betty to be concerned about the show's image, when its workers and performers had been "let loose." Much damage can be done to a touring organization by the antics of its personnel, even though they represent no more than would occur in any average, small town. The fact that the people are on the road is what makes the difference.

But it was equally right for the performers and workers, confined by months of one-day stands on the road, to have the chance to kick over their traces once in a while. The look on Jan Perz's face as he sat in the driver's seat of the truck, about to embark on a drunken trip to take his Polish friend out on Saturday night, was enough to tell me that. The bleary grin told me at once that he shouldn't drive, but it told me, as well, that he had earned his night out, and I wished him well as much as I wished him safety.

But as performance time drew near, everything fell back together again. Jumbo's pole had been replaced, the baby elephants were back in the tent, and the fire eater was soaking his torches prior to his "balley" demonstration. The cookhouse was in full swing, scarcely pausing between breakfast and lunch, and the candy vendors were loading their trays preparatory to their trips through the audience as the show progressed. The crowd was beginning to build, straining at the barricades placed at the front door, and a banner show was beginning to gather steam.

Overhead the sky was brilliant and the wind was crisp. It was circus day, and everyone could feel it. Everyone, that is, except a visiting author, who had found himself magically but exhaustingly involved in the occupation of watchman by default.

Circus Bartok

With temperatures soaring, thunderheads building up overhead mean worry and concern for showmen everywhere.

A full house awaits the opening of Circus Bartok in New Jersey.

Teardown always uncovers a mass of litter that must be cleaned up by volunteers—circus-struck "towners" for the most part.

The Circus Bartok marquee.

Late morning on the Bartok lot, with everything ready to go for the afternoon performance.

Despite mechanization, muscle power is still a must on the lots of mud shows.

Beneath a battered big top, Shandra the elephant snatches a snack after pulling the top to its place for an afternoon show.

Here they come! Performers file into the ring for the opening spec of Circus Bartok.

A plumed parader rides on an elephant's trunk in the Grand Entry parade.

Silhouetted against a blazing sun, workers take a break
before placing the ring under Circus Bartok's tent.

Ryzard performs atop his ladder.

A foot-juggler performs at Circus Bartok.

Daintiness and precision show up well during this wire act on Circus Bartok.

A clown is funnier when he can relate to an audience by being physically close to it, as in Circus Bartok.

Exhausted by his work, a mud-show worker "sacks out"
in a truck cab on the lot.

The "connection" is the walled passageway between the
marquee and the big top.

Circus props often fall naturally into informal "still lifes" when they are left around the lot.

*A sight much loved by all circus fans; the circus "bulls"
round the corner of the tent, ready to rush into the ring
for their act.*

*Clowns usually double in brass on most shows. Here,
Circus Bartok's clown sells programs.*

*Betty and Bunni—two baby elephants, are much admired
on the lot of Circus Bartok.*

Jan Perz, Bartok's performance director and all-round animal trainer, waits for the opening spec to begin.

One of Perz's ursine pupils plugs around the ring on a scooter.

Vlasta, a head-balancer on the high trapeze, was a popular star with Circus Bartok. She moved to the Sells and Gray Circus in 1972.

A garish but popular Circus Bartok attraction was one that featured boa constrictors and crocodilians.

David Bartok, Bunni the elephant, and Circus Bartok trainer Jan Perz pose in the ring with a recalcitrant lion cub.

Bartok's Aztec Bird Fantasy featured a free-flying hawk.

Early evening, before a performance on a broiling hot day.

Loafing backstage between appearances in the Circus Bartok ring.

Jan Perz working a circus "bull" at teardown.

David Bartok, "duded up" for a performance, strolls across the lot accompanied by his ballet-dancing, canine friend. (Photo courtesy Circus Bartok)

Bunni Bartok poses for a publicity shot with her trained liberty horse. (Photo courtesy Circus Bartok)

17
EVERY NOW AND THEN
IT HAPPENS

ON A BALMY morning in 1971, the King Bros. Circus arrived at Weissglas Stadium on Staten Island, New York City. Stadium owners prohibited the erection of a big top, and the circus management allowed the trucks to sit around the lot while decisions were reached about how the show would be set up in open air for the best effect.

I arrived at the location to find show personnel loafing in the area, awaiting the signal to begin work. Giving the lot the once-over, my eye fell upon a young man seated on a bale of canvas. His eyes darted everywhere. His face seemed to search each person that passed nearby and his gaze lingered on the three elephants, just removed from their van, with what could only be interpreted as adulation. It was plain that I was viewing something of a rare sight in the 1970s—a circus-struck kid.

The briefest conversation with him proved my hunch correct. Ray Michner was his name, and he carried in his pocket, like a gold ingot, a telegram from Ringling Bros. Circus that invited him for an interview as a prospective student in its clown college. This he showed to me, folding it carefully and replacing it in his shirt pocket.

Written on Ray's face was the burning desire to join the King Bros. Circus. He glumly explained to me that his family thought it was foolish to be a clown, and that he was being coerced into becoming a counselor at a summer camp. We talked at intervals, between which we watched the fas-

cinating business of circus setup, and visited the animals about the lot. Camels, llamas, ponies, Sicilian donkeys, chimps, a tiger, a lion, a leopard, three elephants, more dogs than one could count, and a group of pink goats with golden horns—all of these were there, and none escaped the gaze of this latterday Toby Tyler.

The sun beat down on us, yet the merest suggestion that we leave the lot to buy a cooling drink at the snack bar nearby brought a look of instant panic to his face, and a quick refusal.

Finally I had taken enough of his single-mindedness, and broke the ice.

"Why don't you go with it?" I asked him.

"Oh, Geeze, I don't dare ask anyone. I mean, they're all so busy and I hate to interrupt, and there's no sign out saying they want help and there seems to be plenty of people working and my parents . . . ."

"Hold it," I answered. "Let's take things one at a time. That way they will be a lot easier."

"Good, good. What'll we take first?" We had been sitting on the ground and Ray jumped up, where he anxiously hovered over me.

"Well that man over there, he's Harry Rawls, and a nicer guy you'll never want to meet. Why don't you go and ask him?"

"Who me? Oh, no. I couldn't. I mean I could never . . ."

I got up and pushed him in Rawls's direction. It took several pushes until he neared the manager, but when he finally arrived within speaking distance, he sidestepped to leave me facing Harry. The manager looked up at me from his canvas chair and said, in his slow, warm drawl, "How's it going? Did you get the material you wanted for your newspaper article?"

"Yes," I answered. "Everything is just fine. But did you know that you've got a kid right there who is practically wetting his drawers, he wants to work with the circus so much?"

Harry turned to Ray and looked him up and down.

"How old are you, son?"

"Eighteen."

"That's legal age in New York, isn't it?"

"Yes."

"Well, we can't just make you do anything. That includes a lot of things, you know. Why don't you go out there and sit at ringside and watch the men in the red jump suits? They're from the prop department, and you see if that sort of work would suit you. Just go on out there and sit on the grass."

"You mean not in a seat?" Ray's voice was shaking.

"Right on the grass. Right at ringside."

I don't suppose that Ray saw a thing for the entire performance, although he certainly looked at everything. But his mind failed to register. He was in the pardonable position of missing the trees because of the forest.

Directly following the afternoon show he came to me to discuss the problem of his parents. It was decided that he should find out what his salary would be, report this to his mother and father, and invite them back to the lot for the evening show. I volunteered any help I could, as a resident of Staten Island who was not connected with the circus.

To say that Ray bounded towards home like an antelope would come close to the greatest understatement in history. Would that the Zacchinis, blasted from their circus cannon, could have equalled his speed. They would have been given lifetime contracts, and open ones, at that!

His return to the lot, however, was more like a cortège, for he brought with him his father and mother. His eagerness was spilling over at every sentence, and he stuttered and stumbled his way through introductions. Finally his father took over.

"Hi. I'm Ray's dad. The way it is is like this. I think he should go, because it is what he wants to do. But his mother—well . . . ."

I turned to the mother, who looked both tragic at the prospective loss of her son, and terrified at her unexpected proximity to the three large elephants standing nearby.

"Wouldn't you like to make it unanimous?" I asked gently.

The poor woman couldn't answer. She simply stood there, simultaneously forlorn and nervous. When I looked at her face, she stared blankly back at me, her expression one of utter misery. She started to answer, but her lip quivered, and she fell silent, staring at the ground.

"Well?" I added, hoping to prod her into communication, at which point I felt that things might go a little better.

"I'm so worried," she said in a voice that was tight and squeaky with concern. "What about all those drunks and queers and gambling and where would he sleep and do they feed him?" She stopped, unable to think of any more horrid possibilities and because her voice was starting to shake again.

"It looks like we've got a problem," said Ray's father calmly.

I couldn't help but agree with him, but neither could I carry the ball any further. I had no vested interest in Ray, except to see him do what perhaps I should have done at eighteen, myself. I was stumped, for I had no answer other than to tell the woman that more degenerates of any description she would care to pick probably existed in a three block radius of her home than among the personnel of King Bros. Circus. I showed her the cleanliness of the equipment (feeling that she was probably of the age that believed in cleanliness being next to Godliness) and pointed to the trim, neat dining tent, with its bright table cloths. I even embarked upon a thoroughly invented description of the working crew's sleeping quarters, hoping it would turn the tide.

Still the downcast face and trembling chin. Still the doleful, Spaniel eyes.

Providence, in the person of Harry Rawls, intervened. He strolled across the lot in the background. "There's Harry," I said to Ray. "Why don't you introduce your folks to him?"

In a flash the boy had tugged his recalcitrant mother to where the manager stood, and parents, son and manager stood in quiet conversation. I knew that if anyone could solve the problem, Harry could. He was the sort of man to whom any mother would yield. Her son would be safe under Harry's guidance. She could tell by the tone of his voice and his manner. These are the arguments that sway mothers, and Harry had all the qualifications.

I went into the arena and sat on the grass, shortly to be joined by an ecstatic Ray, who pointed out his mother and father in the audience.

"Damn. They don't see me. I wish they would look over here so I could wave."

"Give 'em time, Ray," I said.

Throughout the performance I watched the parents. Mrs. Michner staring straight ahead, without reacting to the acts. Her husband, on the other hand, applauded earnestly, and nudged his wife as he chortled at the clowns.

About midway through the performance, Mrs. Michner started applauding, too. Towards the end of the show, she was laughing uproariously at some knockabout clowns on a revolving ladder. She was now totally involved. Her husband nudged her again, and pointed in our direction. They waved excitedly, a wave returned with twice the thrill by their son, and by myself. By now Mrs. Michner adored the show. It *couldn't* present an act that wasn't the best in the world because *her* son was with it. It was *his* circus, therefore *hers* as well.

Harry had done his job well.

So it was that in June, 1971, the circus hired a new hand on Staten Island. More than that, it annexed an entire family of brand new circus fans. The 1970s are supposed to be the years when "doing your thing" is the popular trend; but it always was, of course. In fifteen minutes King Bros. Circus opened a whole new life to a kid who felt it to be a very special circus. It is very likely that this was a very special young man who left town that night, still with a telegram from Ringling Bros. in his pocket.

I had the feeling that he was the sort of person about whom I would be hearing in the future.

King Bros. Circus, Staten Island, N. Y. 1971

"Sacked out" in the shade, prior to an afternoon show.

Workers and part-time "towners" push canvas onto the King Bros. Spool Wagon.

In 1971, pink goats were offered as an exotic (and uncooperative) addition to the King Bros. performance.

Madison Square Garden as it appeared set up for the
100th Anniversary production of Ringling Bros. Circus.

D. W. Washburn becomes "Sparky".

The transformation from D. W. Washburn to "Sparky" being complete, the clown dons immaculate, white gloves as he readies himself for an appearance in the ring.

18
TURNED-ON TALENT

BARNSTORMING AROUND the countryside, often barely able to squeak by financially as they poke their multi-ringed presence into the suburbs, are the smaller circuses of America. Bearing the depreciating tag of "mud shows," they literally slug their way through a season that is so physically hard, so discouraging, so fraught with the dichotomy of public adulation and "official" wariness and mistrust that it becomes an actual wonder that they exist at all.

Deprived of the luxury provided by indoor arenas used by larger shows, mud shows batter about the country carrying their own often tattered and begrimed big tops with them. The lots on which they play may be anything from shopping plaza parking areas to private fields rented for the day by their owners.

Such shows as the Carson and Barnes Circus, Sells and Gray Circus, King Bros. Circus, Royal Wild West Circus, and the Hoxie Bros. Circus (which sports lavender trucks) can be found popping up in resort towns during the spring and summer. Circus Bartok also hits the sawdust trail during the summer season, as does the largest tented show in America today, the Beatty-Cole Bros. Circus. The latter can be termed a mud show only because it is transported by trucks. It is really too large for such a moniker, and does, in fact, play arenas on special occasions.

Mud show management officials are invariably astute, for they supervise an organization that hovers like a wirewalker on the brink of disaster. The property that they own represents hundreds of thousands of dollars. Operating expenses are ruinous, maintenance is difficult and specialized, and labor is hard to find and harder to keep for a full season. These factors, coupled with the dreams of grandeur often held by circus owners, have caused many shows to rise and fall in prosperity, and some to "head for the barn" for good.

An early version of King Bros. Circus grew to become the largest truck show on the road in the 1950s, featuring a handsome street parade as a free feature. It finally collapsed under its own financial weight. Also shuttered was a circus based in the Midwest called Mills Bros., which blasted its way through the East years ago in a razzle-dazzle blaze of panoply, literally bursting with raucous energy and brilliant features. A year later its performance was abbreviated and less colorful, though still good; its tent was full of holes, and its personnel downcast. Finally it was heard from no more. One of its owners has sponsored periods of several weeks with other shows in their tour through the old Mills Bros. territory, an action that illustrates the tenacity of a circus owner's vision. The grasp for glory is always there. Dreams die hard on circus lots.

The burden of worry is as heavy as the cigar smoke in many a circus's front office trailer. That is why the atmosphere inside the ticket wagon is usually low-key and calm. This is far different from the atmosphere just outside the window where the tickets are sold. Here the clamor of the midway charges the air, and anticipation is written on the face of every customer. It is with him still as he crowds into the big top to await the start of the performance.

The Sells and Gray front-office trailer is elaborately lettered.

At the back door of the tent, performers gather in preparation for the beginning of the show. Although they talk of many things, their idle chatter is charged with an anticipation that matches the swelling excitement in the audience.

Performers, too, carry their load of worry, but their attitudes are not at all low-key. Emotionally driven by the lure of the circus ring, their careers consist of short periods of time bathed in public applause, and far longer periods spent earning money by selling souvenirs, candy floss, or other circus staples. This work is referred to as being located "out front" almost as if anything not located within the ring itself doesn't really count. Is is a necessary evil.

Mud show performers often help with the erection and teardown of the circus tent, the placement of seats, and the rigging of their own equipment. They care for their own animals, if they have them, and maintain their own living quarters. They

attend to many extra functions like wardrobe repairs, and often appear in secondary roles in the side show. It is customary for them to appear more than once in the ring using different professional names for each appearance, but this is not a chore undertaken by mud show performers only. On the massive Ringling Bros. Circus, some performers appear as many as six times during one performance. But they do not do "ordinary" tasks like taking tickets or ushering, as they do on small shows.

Laborers on small circuses are paid poorly and are noted for their transient status. Although low salary is partly responsible for this situation, the toughness of a circus laborer's life, with its long hours and often miserable working and living conditions, also plays a part. Never really clean, the circus laborer usually sleeps in an "adapted" freight van in the company of all the other laborers on the show. Small window holes along each side of the van provide ventilation from head to foot of the laborer's narrow bunk. It can be imagined that such a metal trailer rig, sitting in the broiling sun all day, affords little comfort except for a relatively soft place to sleep. It is often humid, smelly, and stifling. For this reason, many laborers carry air mattresses and small tents that they set up in shady spots around the lot. Some prefer to sleep in truck cabs.

For the performer, life is better. Because a circus artist commands a salary that is at least reasonable (and often much more than that), he can live under conditions that support his health and comfort. Living conditions must furnish him with the proper place to prepare for his appearance, store his props, and maintain a level of cleanliness that permits him to appear fresh and full of vigor in the ring. Gleaming trailers parked around the lot testify to the personal success of their inhabitants.

Many a performer also owns a home in the town where the circus winter quarters are located, but nearly every show person prefers the quasi-vagabond life of the road. It is more a matter of form than fact that a circus performer complains constantly about his unsettled life.

The core of the circus is its performance. The verve and drive that makes a show "go" is largely up to the performer. That he possesses an almost demented zeal can be seen by looking at the conditions under which he must often operate, and murderous schedule to which he must adhere. To the performer, the most tawdry canvas arena is transformed into a ring of glory merely by his or her presence, a feat that comes as close to magic as anything can in the twentieth century.

Look again at the aerial star, perched on her trapeze at the top of a stifling hot, mud show circus tent. She is not, in fact, the bone-tired, stringy-haired girl in patched net hose that she appears to be. For her precious five or ten minutes aloft she glitters. She literally reigns over the sea of up-turned faces that surround her in the seats below. This is *her* moment; and we are with her all the way, believing in her talents, hoping that the ropes won't break, and urging her on to ever more reckless manipulations.

Not only is she "turned on," but she has turned on the entire audience as well!

As she clambers down the rope ladder or slides to the earth along a single "web" to the accompaniment of cheers from the bleachers, one wonders about the ridiculous talk of the circus as a dying institution. When one mud show after another continually plays to jammed, excited audiences, the future of the circus in America seems more secure than publicist-philosophers would have us believe.

The reason? Turned-on talent, that yearly helps the circus reach for its advertised goal—to be bigger and better than ever.

These design photographs are from the private collection of the designer Miles White, and are published here for the first time with his permission. During the time that White designed and costumed Ringling spectacles, he brought the creation of allegorical floats to a remarkable level of taste and originality.

The spectacle for which these sketches were executed was called The Good Old Times. *It was filmed on location at the circus in 1951 for Cecil B. DeMille's Paramount epic,* The Greatest Show on Earth.

"American Beauties" float as it came directly from the imagination of the internationally famous designer Miles White. This preliminary sketch is without regard for scale. (Author's photo)

The same idea worked into spectacular reality. (Author's photo)

*White's masterly and fanciful sketch for a "Sleeping
Beauty" float saw many changes before it was completed.
(Author's photo)*

*The finished product, although vastly different, was a
beauty. (Author's photo)*

"Moonlight Melodies" came from the lively White mind as a baroque fantasy with classical allusions. (Author's photo)

As constructed, it lost some of the delicacy of its designer's feeling, and appeared somewhat modernized. But it was a success on its own terms. (Author's photo)

"CBS" meant Circus Broadcasting Studio. (Author's photo)

Miles White's sketch in finished form saw size relationships altered, and some original ideas discarded. The CBS letters are upside down for safe storage and transport of the jeep-mounted float. (Author's photo)

The icicle-garbed stairway held a circus queen on the White-designed beauty. The sconcelike "arms" beside the mirror top held pen-lite "candles" that were forever getting lost or broken while the circus was on tour. (Author's photo)

A flamboyant example of Miles White's fertile imagination—and of Ringling excess. This inoperative calliope simply sat in a ring as the rest of the lavish spectacle passed by. (Author's photo)

White's costume sketches are often masterpieces. (Author's photo)

A White conception of a walk-on costume for an aerial star. Such a costume was worn by Betty Hutton in the film The Greatest Show on Earth. *(Author's photo)*

The tragedy of such handsome costumes as are used for entrances is that they are briefly seen before being cast off so that the aerialist can perform unencumbered by bulky magnificence. (Author's photo)

19

BEARS IN THE RING

THE FORERUNNERS OF trained bears as we know them in circuses were undoubtedly the dancing bears that performed in European village streets under the control of their gypsy owners. Little did spectators at those entertainments realize that the "jolly bears" that reared onto their hind legs at the sound of the tambourine had been trained with vicious cruelty as cubs. The animals, their vision often impaired for life by trainers, regarded the sound of the tambourine as a warning to keep their forefeet held high; the same sound had formerly resulted in seared paws when the animals placed them on heated metal plates as they returned to all fours during their "training periods." Such ghastly pain associated with a tambourine quickly taught them to remain upright whenever its dreaded sound was heard.

Although no reports of cruel treatment equal to that employed by the Romanies exist in the garbled records of circus training, bears have consistently been regarded as "tough customers" when carried with any circus. If some members of a performing troupe are unduly recalcitrant, they are simply forced to perform. Forcing a bear to do anything at all is like ordering a stone wall to move, and overpowering a monster bruin must be done physically, if the animal resists suggestion, coaxing, or bribes. This is not easy, for bears are immensely strong animals, well insulated against blows by thick fur and solid skulls. Some trainers believe that bears cannot be disciplined by a human unless the trainer is armed.

According to one authority, bears are best trained by discovering what they do best naturally, and adapting a routine to suit the animal's traits. Another expert argues that it would be as deplorable *not* to reward a bear for its performance as it would be *to* reward a lion or tiger. Regardless of a trainer's approach, there is no guarantee that the bear will enjoy performing such a trick at a given time.

A name that is still remembered in connection with circus bears is that of Emil Pallenberg. Bears presented under his tutelage were always something special to audiences because they did what their trainer bade them to do unfailingly, and with great style. The truth of the matter was that Pallenberg was schooled in the early German style of hard, rough training at Hagenbeck's before Willy Hagenbeck introduced the approach to animal training known as "gentle schooling." The results that Pallenberg obtained were remarkable, but the image presented was sometimes false. Failure to execute a trick properly in the Pallenberg troupe meant enduring the master's violent discipline, and every bear knew this.

Such is the dogged nature of a bear's "personality" that the animal often nurtures grudges, remaining below the boiling point as it builds up resentment until finally it becomes permanently vindictive, with murder paramount on its mind. A bear in this condition bites at everything—cage bars, performing pedestals, food trays, and everything that comes within reach. It is not long for the ring. Perhaps this is why bear trainers are noted for their injuries, and consider the performing career of their charges to be short compared to other circus animals.

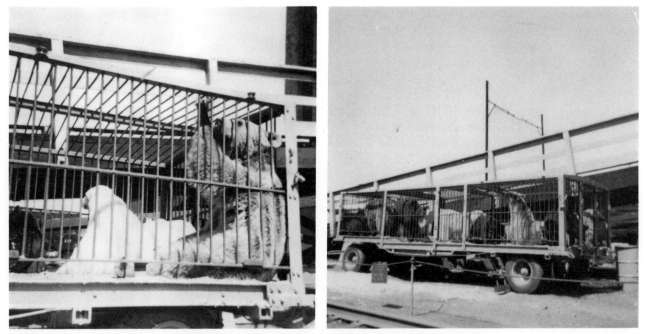

Albert Rix's large group of performing bears performed together and lived together as well. (Author's photos)

Mixing different species of bears is a tremendous feat, and one that can take as long as two months to accomplish. It was in 1950 that Albert Rix, another Hagenback protégé, appeared with an elaborately schooled, large group of bears in Ringling's center ring. His act featured many species of bears, and replaced the traditional cat act for several years. It was the first time that American audiences had seen bears presented in an arena cage, and the first time that they had witnessed so many performing together. The act, which furnished exotic background material for the Cecil B. DeMille film *The Greatest Show on Earth,* featured a huge, brown bear that remained on its hind legs during the entire presentation, rotating about in the cage. The hind-leg walker paused only to place a paw on Rix's shoulder, or to buss him sloppily on the nose.

Smaller groups of bears were shown in succeeding years by several circuses. The first visit of the Moscow Circus brought Constantin Filatov, whose "bear circus" occupied the entire second half of the program. Many bears were used in this act, but they were brought out in quick succession, and never entered the ring all at the same time. America's second visit from the Soviets brought Gosha —a solitary bear that not only rode a motorcycle, but that actually drove it. The immense beast steered the machine twice around the ring follow-

ing its trainer, who rode another cycle. When the trainer left the ring, Gosha took another spin around, then steered its vehicle out of the arena, dumbfounding and delighting audiences.

A further visit from the Russians involved the Moscow Circus On Ice (successful neither as circus or ice show, but charming in its own way). Included in its roster of performers was a troupe of bears that played hockey on ice skates! The act was a shambles as a hockey game, but successful as a bear act.

Over the years, Klauser's Bears, Konselman's Bears and Hawthorne's Bears have been among the bear acts that have been seen by many circusgoers. Sometimes these acts were presented with Ringling and sometimes with Shrine circuses.

Few smaller circuses exhibited bear acts, because bears can be genuine trouble on back lots as well as in the ring. The Cristiani Circus was an exception. Circus Bartok always featured a bear act in its single ring, usually under the expert tutelage of Jan Perz, the Polish trainer originally featured with Ringling Bros. Circus. Perz developed a trick in which a bear walked a flight of stairs on its hind legs to an elevated pedestal, then performed a "nose stand" using nose and front legs only, as the pedestal revolved. As seen on a one-ring show, the act was sensational, for the animal was not more than twenty feet from spectators. It was even closer to them as it rode a scooter and, finally, a motorcycle around the ring. Unlike many other trainers, Perz allowed his bruins complete liberty in the ring. Similarly, his act required no attendants who stood beside bears when they were not performing. A simple clip lead was all that held the animals to their ringside seats, a fact as remarkable as any of the tricks that they performed.

In 1970, Ringling Bros. Circus brought a new bear act to America. It came from the famed Circus Althoff in Germany and was trained and exhibited by one of that illustrious family's own members, Jacki Althoff. At that time he showed a troupe of seven bears in the ring—an unusually large number for a routine that was not presented within the confines of an arena cage.

One of the seven was an escape artist, much to the annoyance of the circus management. At least twice during one of the circus' New York City stands, a young Canadian black bear bolted like greased lightning from the ring, shot across a nearby ring full of chimpanzees (that fled *en masse* to the arms of their trainers) and disappeared through the back door. Each time the recaptured defector was returned ceremoniously to the ring.

Jacki's act is showy and spectacular, but the appearance of friendliness and togetherness that seems true in the ring is entirely false. Bears are simply not built so that they can be treated that way, according to Althoff. Beyond much doubt, the escape artist was due for a reprimand.

In 1971, three American brown bears (of which the regional type called the grizzly is the most famous) dominated the Althoff act. The remaining four bears were Canadian blacks—only one of which was truly black. Although Jacki claimed his bears to be grizzlies (and, in a sense, he was correct) they did not show the light-tipped hairs that are the trademarks of grizzly bears. They were certainly as impressive as grizzlies as far as size went, and gave the impression of approaching the size of the famed Kodiak bears that come from the island near Alaska.

Like most circus performers interviewed, Althoff blushed as he apologized for his lack of command over the English language.

"If you ask a man what to train is the most hardest, it is always the bear. You ask a man which is worse—tiger or bear—and he will take five tigers to one bear. Give me tiger, he says.

"The big one in the act, he put me in hospital two times already. Everyone think that bears is nice; but they is not. The trouble is with the kids. They have always the teddy bear, and go like this (Jacki cradled his arms and pretended to put a teddy bear to sleep), but they have no tiger teddy bear—no lion teddy bear. That's no good. Bears is tough. In Europe we have only two people with bears. Myself is one, and Roberts is other. He uses four bears; but next year I may add two. Others are always in hospital, or dead, or quit bears."

I was becoming a bit edgy, for I had been talking outside Althoff's trailer as he was preparing the monster animals for their entrance into the ring. They were, I felt, getting a bit too close for comfort. Nevertheless, I continued.

"What about the intelligence of bears?"

"From alles animals, I think bears is the most smart."

"But their expression is so deadpan. Can you tell what their mood is like?"

"Oh, ja! The people say you cannot tell, but I can tell. When I get them out of the cage, I can tell is he mad or lazy—if he is nervous or no nervous. I see this. I don't care what people say."

"What about the diet of your troupe," I asked.

"They eat in a week 200 bread, one hundred pounts carrot, and fifty pounts salad."

There was a pause as Jacki surveyed the enormous bruins weaving back and forth, impatient for their trip to the ring.

"But you know I tell you something. The older the bear, the more crazy. I work with the big one maybe three, four years; but the older he is, the more crazy, the more dangerous.

"People say to me when I tell them I try to train grizzlies, you are crazy. Like a bear you are crazy. But now you see I do it, and no one else does it, and I am with Ringling!"

At a *very* respectful distance, I followed the Althoff contingent to the ring where I saw the astounding sight of three grizzlies operating a seesaw, one walking a huge ball up a spiral incline while balancing atop the ball on its hind legs, and smaller bears pushing each other about in perambulators, dashing on front feet only around the ring curb, and doing all sorts of odd feats.

Several were at liberty in the ring, while others were exhibited on long leads. But differences in their training now seemed clear to me, or at least I thought so. Some seemed to work out of fear of punishment if they did not perform well. Others, more casual in actions, seemed to perform secure in the knowledge that a trick well done would warrant a later reward.

I was curious about the days when the act was not shown, for many show animals stiffen, and become unduly nervous when they don't work. After the bears had completed their turn in the ring, I asked Althoff how the animals' temperaments were after a day's layover.

"Ha! After a day off the bears is better!" (Jacki stood and flexed his muscles to illustrate the point, although he was pouring sweat from his recently finished performance.)

"They come out and seem like to say—'Hey! lemme out so I can run around and perform!'—but after seven days straight of performance and work they are bad. A little lazy on the edges, like people."

Like most people, maybe, but not like Jacki Althoff. He left abruptly to prepare for one of his three appearances in the circus "specs" and to take care of his hundreds of chores involving the backstage care of bears. He looked—well—a little like a bear himself.

20

THOSE WERE THE DAYS

AMONG OLD-TIME sights surely gone forever are those magnificent animals, the draft horses. Only periodic appearances of show teams now occur, and when they do, they draw enormous crowds, for the impression of these huge animals is always sensational.

The circus formerly boasted numerous draft horses, for all of the shows not traveling by rail moved by horsepower in its truest sense. Even railroad shows used draft horses to load and unload their flatcars, sixty years or so ago, and carried up to three hundred horses just for that purpose.

Since the circus always likes to show itself off, the custom became to use matched teams of roans, blacks, and grays. It was Ringling that popularized the dappled gray Percheron. The show did so by keeping two studs in their winter quarters from 1884 until 1918. These stallions were in great demand by breeders, for Ringling was always in the market for horses that were dappled gray in color. The show "sold" the stud services of its magnificent stallions, then bought the offspring. Much later, in the 1950s, Percherons were used by that show in a remarkable liberty routine in the center ring.

In the freight department, large teams of horses were often used, owing to the weight of the massive baggage wagons. In street parades, teams of eight or ten horses were not uncommon, but more horses were added for display. Perhaps the most famous of all such parade teams was the forty-horse hitch used by Ringling Bros. Circus.

Unusual chores were sometimes delegated to circus draft horses. A novel example of this occurred when a four-horse hitch on the Orrin Bros. Circus was required to pull an elephant's tooth! The ulcerated molar was causing the show's elephant giant-size misery, so the beast was chained to the ground and its trunk tied onto its back. The gum of the tooth was soaked in cocaine and a three-quarter-inch hole was drilled through the offending molar. A rope tied to a bar was inserted, and fastened to the lead bar of the horse team. When the team began pulling, the elephant reared in protest. The action caused the rotting tooth to pop out, and the elephant to land on its rump!

The horse remained as motor power in a more ordinary sense for many years on the circus. Stock was carefully tended and constantly checked for injury or strain. A special tent housed the draft stock, and was not usually open to the public. Rainy weather called for the erection of sidewalls, thereby affording total protection for these valuable animals.

On railroad shows, baggage stock was loaded fully harnessed. Each was placed close to another, to prevent the animals from lying or being thrown down. Once loaded, the bit was removed from each horse's mouth. A chain fastened to an overhead pipe was fixed to the horse's collar, removing the collar's weight from the horse itself. An "S" hook of soft metal held the collar so that if the horse did get thrown to the floor, the hook straightened itself out and released itself.

Driving a large team presented special problems. Jake Posey, famed driver of the forty-horse hitch used when Ringling Bros. went to Europe,

The "new" Schlitz 40-horse hitch. Forty Belgian draft horses, four abreast, ten deep, walked down the streets of Milwaukee in the 1972 Schlitz Circus Parade, the first occasion that a 40-horse hitch had been seen since 1904. Dick Sparrow, a farmer and horse breeder from Zearing, Iowa, drove the huge team over a three-mile route before an estimated 600,000 people. The Schlitz Forty made a return engagement for the 1973 parade. (Courtesy Don Dooley, Old Milwaukee Days)

had a brake man and an assistant to keep the lines straight. Rounding a corner, twenty feet of lines slid through his fingers. When the team straightened out, his assistant pulled the lines back through his hands again. The lead lines on this incredible team were 120 feet long. Altogether, 3420 feet of lines were used to pull a massively handsome bandwagon called The Two Hemispheres.

It was a real sight, massive and spectacular, as the matched team of bays, four abreast, clattered down the street. I suppose that is what is remembered as the good old days; but Posey, who sprained both wrists more than once while driving teams, is a more important symbol of those times. They were hard. Very hard.

The good old days? They weren't that easy!

21
JACKPOTTING
WITH BILLY BAKER

AMONG HORSE TRAINERS active in circus work in the 1970s, England's Billy Baker and his son Tommy are among the very best. Baker has trained horses on every major show in the world, and counts his work with the famed Circus Schumann in Denmark as one of his more important experiences. Schumann (later sold to become Circus Beneweiss) was known all over the world for its magnificent horses; they were its leading attraction. Baker is a former Bertram Mills horse trainer, too. When the Mills show closed, he went with its horses to Mexico and took over horse displays for that country's Circus Atayde. It was from that engagement that Billy came to Ringling in America. He has now trained horses for both the Red and Blue units of the circus.

"How many horses have you ever handled at once," I asked Billy, as we sandwiched ourselves between sequined capes, bodies, plumed hats, and other dressing room accoutrements backstage in New York City.

"Sixteen. I tried sixteen once; but you gotta run 'em double if you use that many. There's no room because of the ring, you see. But a nice number is eight. You can run 'em fast if you've got eight. You know, changes, pirouettes and all that. Twelve is a really high number, a hard number to hold, to do a nice routine with. Jeanette Williams, on the Red Unit, has twelve; but they're pretty hard to hold because they're stallions; and they 'ave a go at one another, you know. I've got a few stallions in my grays on the Blue Unit, too, and they'll have a go at it, too. You've gotta watch 'em, and check 'em. But ring size has a lot to do with it. I'd say we 'ave about a forty-foot ring 'ere. When you're on earth, a forty-two-foot ring makes it so that twelve 'orses is about the nice number.

"You know, this year I took over the Blue Unit 'orses in the month between seasons. You can't do that and get perfect results first off. When you go into the ring with twelve new grays like me and Tommy did, they're all alike at first. Even though the 'orses is already trained, you might say; you don't really get the feel of it for about—oh—a couple o' months on the road. By then you know every movement; and with twelve you don't get that in a week or two weeks. Every 'orse is an individual, like people. They've got their little faults, and you've got to watch out for them. In a little while a trainer catches every fault individually; and you call 'is name—bang! You've got 'im. Some of the 'orses here got names like Castro, David, Rex, Tunis, Bingo, Beirut, Omaha, Hemio —when you call an 'orse in the ring you've gotta give 'im a short name, because you can't go calling him Sisslewell, or something like that. You've got to get 'is attention fast."

"What about green horses, horses that have never seen any form of performance training? How do you start out? What's the first thing you teach a horse like that?" I asked.

"You ring 'im. That's what you do. You take

'im into the ring on a long lunge and you run 'im 'round one way, and then stop 'im, and run 'im 'round the other. Then you stop 'im, and make 'im come to you.

"Green 'orses are sometimes wonderful. Once, when we were in Africa, we 'ad an 'orse sickness, and we lost three. So I went out into the bush. Actually, it was in Zululand. I called one of the 'orses Zulu, matter o' fact. I paid, well, I paid just about nothing for 'im, something like twenty pounds. The 'orse was so green we 'ad to rope 'im and bring 'im in. He was really wild. Well that little 'orse—all three of 'em, really—they were so smart and so intelligent. They broke to training so quickly it was a beautiful thing to see. We didn't 'ave trucks or caravans in Africa. We stayed on the trains, and I used to train the new 'orses in the runs alongside the railroad tracks."

"OK. Let's get back to training. You say you train him to go each way around the ring, and train him to come up to you. What next?"

"Oh, that's only for a liberty 'orse. We 'ave what we call Rosinbacks. They're for the acrobats to ride in the bareback routine. Now you never train a Rosinback to go two ways. He always goes in the same direction. You break 'im by walking 'im 'round the ring until he gets the feel of it; and then you break 'im *not* to trot. You break 'im straight into a canter. A Rosinback can run false, or out of gait; and that causes the acrobats to mess up their stunts on 'is back. With liberty 'orses it doesn't matter, because there's no one on top to worry about. Sometimes it takes longer to train a Rosinback than to train a liberty 'orse. You gotta train a Rosinback's riders, too. They've gotta ride 'im light, so'se he'll take the weight, and use the flip of 'is rump to help them do their stunts. Rosinback riders can get an 'orse so'se they can ride up 'is neck, and go over 'is ears and drop in front of 'im. You've gotta make an 'orse like that so'se he doesn't shy. You bring obstacles so'se any movement from the fans won't scare 'im, or any flash cameras, or anything like that.

"A good Rosinback is not found very often. Once a rider's got a good 'orse, and got 'im trained—money could never buy 'im.

"Buying a Rosinback, or a Jockey 'orse, as we call 'em, is a very critical thing. Some guys get 'em too heavy, but you've gotta buy what's available. But a good buy would be an 'orse that's got what we call the weight in bone. You feel the bones of the leg. You couldn't use a Jockey 'orse routine on a liberty 'orse, or an Arabian. You'd kill a liberty 'orse that way.

"Ponies, now that's another thing. Ponies—oh, they're really sons of . . . —they're terrible things. My son Tommy, 'ere, he's a pony man, bless 'im. But I'd rather show twenty 'orses than two ponies! The ponies with the Red unit—you know—the ones with the sulkies—they're good. I done a routine with 'em. They do splits, changes, everything in the book. There are twelve of 'em, and I don't think there's a set of ponies in the world as good as the Ringling ponies.

"Those long whips we use—you call 'em ring whips—is mostly used for showmanship and cues. They're pointers, really. Once you've got the hang of 'ow an 'orse is broke, and 'ow the breaker pointed with 'is whip, you've got it licked.

"But like I say, the riding 'orse, that's the 'ard one to break, and nobody knows it. They think you just put 'im in the ring and let 'im run around and it's easy. But it's not. Here's a true story.

"We met this man who said he'd make a Jockey 'orse for us; and we told 'im all about 'ow 'ard it is, and what you've gotta do to make 'im so'se he won't shy, and carry a rider regular and all; and we bet 'im he couldn't do it—but he said he could. Well, allright, we says. We'll be back next year and see. Well, wouldn't you know, we went back next year *and he 'ad one!* He didn't 'ave a ring curb like we do, so he made one of bales of straw and 'ay; and the bloke really did make a riding 'orse—BUT—he broke it to run the opposite way! I'd bet every penny on it, that you send our Rosinback riders here on the Ringling show into the ring on an 'orse running the opposite way, and they wouldn't stand up more than once 'round the ring! That's because the riders are trained, too, you see. The whole rhythm and bounce is different. It just never works.

"But 'ow many really good Rosinbacks do you have in the life of a bareback rider? You could count 'em on two fingers. Justino Loyal, a great name in riding, with a famous career—he 'ad only one really good 'orse. And Pete Cristiani, who did some fabulous tricks on a Rosinback, did them only on one 'orse, as I remember it. When they lost the 'orse he stopped doing some of 'is tricks, the same as Justino Loyal."

"So it's Rosinbacks, not liberty horses, that show the greatest achievements in horse training among the free-running horse acts in the circus?" (I was deliberately omitting the whole subject of *haute école,* or high school horses, when I asked the question.)

"Definitely. No question about it," said Billy, as he reached for his sequined waistcoat and herded me towards the door. Spec time was approaching, and spare time, used for gossiping ("jackpotting" in circus parlance) was at an end.

"And ponies?"

"Aacchh! You can keep 'em. Talk to my son Tommy about 'em, if you want; but as for me, I 'aven't a decent word to say about 'em!"

22

HOXIE HOLIDAY

WINDING ITS WAY from Florida through a tour of 13 to 15 states yearly is another of the tented circuses familiar to patrons on the East Coast. While not the largest circus under canvas (a title claimed by the impressive Beatty-Cole Circus) Hoxie Bros. Circus, famed for its purple trucks and fast-paced, winning performance, was steadily climbing to a point of prominence in 1972, when its tour led it on a circuitous route back and forth through Florida, Georgia, South Carolina, North Carolina, Virginia, Kentucky, Ohio, Michigan, and as far west as Illinois. Crossing back to the coast it played Indiana, Ohio, West Virginia, Pennsylvania, a group of short moves in nearby New Jersey, back to Pennsylvania and ended its 29-week tour in Central City of that state some time in the month of October. It was a season that started out with miseries for tented circuses everywhere. Torrential rains brought flooding conditions and high winds that caused more than one blowdown, and, in some instances, stranded circuses on flood-surrounded islands. Hoxie and Betty Tucker persisted in their pursuit of this battle against the elements, and brought the show through with a winning tour. They were helped immeasurably in this by the publication of the Hoxie Circus story in the National Geographic Magazine, March 1972.

As one of the larger tented circuses, Hoxie Bros. boasts a "cat act" featuring lions and tigers. The act, a peppery combination of skill, ferocity, and bravado is announced as having "America's foremost trainer of jungle beasts—Prince Bogino!" The prince, entering the steel arena replete with turban, sequin-splashed jacket and silver-spangled pants, is called Junior on the lot. His name is really Manuel Ruffin. He learned his craft from Clyde Beatty, and had been performing on his own for fifteen years in 1972. He is the much-needed mechanic of Hoxie Bros. Circus, as well as one of its feature attractions.

I have always enjoyed the Hoxie elephant acts. One of these featured two baby African elephants presented as a schooling session and the other, featuring the larger elephants, employed the flippantly informal services of Tom Armstrong's large, black dog, that raced and yapped its way around the ring looking for all the world like a stray that had wandered into the tent by mistake, until it jumped wildly onto an elephant's back and barked loudly at the audience. Armstrong, it seemed to me, presented a personally unique bull act—loose and fun-filled, but remarkable for its skill and humor. His was unlike the Beatty-Cole bull act, where the speed and intensity of the circus's thundering herd gave the awesome impression of brutal power. Armstrong's act with Hoxie differed, too from the high-style, precision routines of Ringling's bulls under Gautier or Schmitt.

For the 1973 season Armstrong was provided with an increased herd of 10 elephants. It is through visible proof of wealth, as in the case of larger elephant herds, that the average circus-goer knows when a show is doing well. But there are other signs of this besides elephants.

In 1973 John Hall, Hoxie Bros. Circus manager, broke with circus tradition and designed a tent that displayed three rings and three stages

"Prince" Bogino faces a charging lioness that actually enjoys the performance as much as its trainer. (Photo courtesy John Hall, Hoxie Bros. Circus)

Joyce Fox, a university graduate, was Hoxie Bros. Circus's all-round circus girl in 1969 and 1970. (Photo courtesy John Hall, Hoxie Bros. Circus)

Hoxie and Betty Tucker pose with two African elephant babies. (Photo courtesy John Hall, Hoxie Bros. Circus)

Hoxie's elephant, Bonnie, raises a Hoxie circus tent. (Photo by Mel Olsen)

not in linear succession, as had been the custom throughout circus history, but arranged in triangular fashion. In between each ring was placed a stage, while the rear stage consisted of the steel arena for Prince Bogino's lions and tigers. In order to permit maximum visibility for the audience, the arena cage was backed, at the tent's sidewall, by the bandstand. The hippodrome track, surrounding the rings, was circular, rather than oval—a shape that was followed through by the shape of the tent itself. No reserved seats were sold inside the tent—another feature that seems to make the Hoxie Bros. Circus unique among tented shows. The strongest point in favor of this departure from circus tradition was that while it permitted exhibition of as large a show as Hoxie had ever presented, it kept performers close to the audience, and retained the intimacy of a tented circus that makes it what it is. Higher and wider than any other circus tent in the United States, its shape permitted it to fit into available lots that could not house a long, oval-shaped tent.

So it was that in 1973, the massive, blue and white dome of Hoxie Bros. Circus's new "canvas coliseum" was raised in circus lots along the route, proof positive that the tented circus was not dead in America.

23

BIGGER AND BETTER THAN EVER— IS IT REALLY?
(A personal opinion)

WELL, IS IT? When the golden phrases slip from the ring announcer's voice, and we are told that the riches of the earth are about to spew forth especially for us; should we really believe him?

In my opinion, if the circus is not bigger than ever, it is markedly better. Talent such as never before now appears before us simply as a matter of course. A case in point was the "flying horse" used in the finale of Ringling's 101st edition. The act consisted of a white horse, ridden by the show's star equestrienne, which mounted a platform. The platform was then hoisted high into the air as production filled the rings surrounding it. As effective as the stunt was, it had the feeling of an effect, rather than a feat, because better talent was exhibited (even by the rider) in the same show. Ringling wisely relegated the act to a finale feature, rather than making it a solo routine earlier in the performance. In the old days, when the flying horse routine first appeared, it caused a sensation.

Personally I feel that emphasis on quantity, rather than quality, does not contribute to the development of the circus as an art. (Of course it seems to pull in plenty of customers, so it must contribute to the survival of the circus as a business.) Quantity simply cannot be maintained now as it used to be, for the cost is prohibitive. Those who have been "circusing" for a long enough time will respond with a yawn to the announcement that the largest herd of performing elephants is about to enter when they know it to number some twenty-odd animals. They feel a little let down, because they can remember fifty-five making the garden shake. The line of elephants used to be so long that it was still entering the arena as the first elephant in the file made its exit. But at the same time it should be noted that the Feld management of Ringling Bros. Circus has assembled three herds of elephants. One is used on each of the Red and Blue Units and one is to be featured in Ringling's circus-themed park located in Florida. All three herds together number somewhere around 60 elephants.

In my opinion, production should serve performance. The tendency of many circuses to "dress" a performance in order to make it look more opulent or larger than it is, seems to be emphasis in the wrong area. The American circus is not alone in this trait. A foreign case in point appears in some French circuses, where they often pad their performances with ballet sequences, some of them hopeless from the point of view of both the circus and the ballet!

Created years ago, the Ringling aerial ballet caused much comment when it first appeared. Over the years, however, it seems to have become a vehicle for production, rather than for a center-ring feature *supported* by production. To reawaken my interest it would have to be dramatically altered and improved. But the Felds, as new producers of the circus, just happen to be the right people to perform exactly that miracle, for they instituted a "skyrousel" that carried aerialists around aloft, merry-go-round fashion, in their 102nd edition of the circus. Unfortunately the apparatus (which must have been a wonder) was too cumbersome and faltering to complete the 1972 tour.

I was surprised that the Felds had not created a one-ring circus by 1972. Every performer that I have spoken to yearns for such a showcase; and the idea is spreading like a brushfire among the circus-going public as well, undoubtedly spurred by the several successful visits of the unique and brilliant Moscow Circus. The Felds have at their fingertips the ingredients for a one-ringer that would be unequalled anywhere on earth. On Ringling's Blue Unit alone, an excellent roster could be assembled; Charly Baumann and his tigers, Billy and Tommy Baker and their horses and ponies, the fabulous Stephensons with their high-styled dog review and, as the Riding Saxons, with their bareback riding act, and the exhilarating Geonas as aerialists. Having purchased the elephant herd from England's Billy Smart's Circus in 1972, the Felds could well supply a smaller herd of circus "bulls" for a one-ring unit. Such a circus would undoubtedly be the choicest show in the entire history of the circus anywhere in the world, far outranking its nearest competitor in the calibre of its unparalleled perfection. It would be the ultimate circus.

The circus is better than it used to be; and it is, at the same time, not as big. It is simply different. If it is not the same, there is no reason why it should be. It is a different time and a different place; and the circus plays to different audiences. But audiences now, as in earlier times, are impressed and entertained by the wonder of human and animal performers doing incredible things. The collective pulse of a circus audience still quickens at the boom of a bass drum and the shriek of the equestrian director's whistle. It always will, because the circus is *special*. When the houselights plunge the arena into darkness, or when the band strikes up beneath a canvas top, the effect is the same. The circus has begun, and all else dims from the circus fan's mind.

I am tempted to agree with e. e. cummings, who hit the nail on the head when he wrote "Damn everything but the circus!"

INDEX